The Best
of Babbie

The wicked wisdom
of Babbie Tongren,
the Afghan Hound's
greatest wit

AN AFGHAN HOUND REVIEW BOOK • REVODANA PUBLISHING

REVODANA PUBLISHING
81 Lafayette Avenue, Sea Cliff, N.Y. 11579

ISBN: 978-1-943824-02-1

www.revodanapublishing.com

This book is dedicated to my sisters, Carol and Honi, for their encouragement and support in making this first volume of Afghan Hound history possible. And to all our wonderful Afghan Hounds, who have enriched our lives. And, of course, to Babbie, for leaving us these memories. — *Fran Reisman*

TABLE OF CONTENTS

Introduction

There were some very great women who took over Afghan Hound breeding in the United States in the 1940s and '50s, continuing on into the 1980s. They were known by their first names to those of us who sat by them: Sunny, Kay, Reigh and Babbie …

Where would our breed be without all four? Each had her own theories, her own ways, but all loved this breed and blessed us by teaching us why they felt the way they did, and why Afghan Hounds became the center of their lives.

Babbie Tongren – or Ruth, as she demanded of those she didn't favor – was the sharp-witted, impatient, dramatic, one-sentence sister. She was always ready to teach from her own book of Afghan Hounds, but you'd better listen, or not only was your lesson over, but you'd be walking away not knowing what hit you when she was through telling you what she really thought of you.

But Babbie was also kind and caring. Our favorite Babbie story was when our brother, who was a young innocent at the time, told her that he was never included in the cards that would come to the house for his sisters. They were always addressed to "Carol, Honi, Fran and the Hounds." He guessed that he must have been the Hounds. From then, on he received cards from Babbie addressed solely to him.

As much as Babbie believed in the beauty and importance of Afghan Hounds, she also believed in the rights of people. She was, more often than not, in hot water with the Afghan Hound Club of America for what she believed was the insensitivity shown by its board toward her fellow Afghan Hound people. Never one to take anything sitting down, she fought for her beliefs, failing to meet the requirement of silence that was expected at the time.

Her wit drew the brightest of dog people to her side, no matter where she was – and she was everywhere. She judged dogs at a time when you could show levity in the ring without the AKC breathing down your neck.

She believed strongly in her "ben ghaZi" Afghan Hounds. She loved the puppies that her stud dogs sired, and she championed the people who were "smart enough" to breed to these dogs. But she also saw the value in dogs from other lines. Certainly her breeding to Sunny Shay's Grandeur line gave her exactly what she expected and what she wanted.

Babbie was admired by many. Her judging extended from Afghans to all hounds to many other breeds. People throughout the sport appreciated her opinion and made her one of the "A Group" at dog show events.

I sometimes wish that aside from leaving beautiful pedigrees that Babbie and her three Afghan sisters – Sunny Shay of Grandeur Afghan Hounds, Kay Finch of Crown Crest Afghan Hounds and Reigh Abram of Dureigh Afghan Hounds – had been able to leave something of themselves to better the future of dog shows.

Babbie "on call." This photo accompanied her articles in *Afghan Hound Review.* *Photo courtesy Sighthound Review/Bo Bengtson*

In Babbie's case, you are holding that legacy in your hands –words of wicked wisdom that appeared in the pages of *Afghan Hound Review* magazine in the 1970s well into the 1980s. Sometimes scolding, sometimes sentimental, each column never failed to educate and entertain.

"I think of her as the Dorothy Parker of the dog world," says fellow breeder and Babbie confidante Richard Souza of Coastwind Afghan Hounds, referring to the famed Algonquin Table writer who once quipped that the first thing she did in the morning was "brush my teeth and sharpen my tongue." "No one ever said it like Babbie. No one ever will."

After reading this collection of her best and brightest columns, most would be hard pressed to disagree.

Fran Reisman
Publisher
Afghan Hound Review

Chapter 1

And So Began the Saga

"All my life I've wanted an Afghan."

A barefaced lie! The truth is, I'd never given it a thought. Those carelessly spoken words catapulted me right up to one of those dangerous corners where our destinies depend upon which turn we take.

A group of us had been to a movie in which a pair of Afghans were featured, and later we stopped at our friendly neighborhood watering hole, where we were joined by a young man who'd been to the same picture. It soon became obvious that the rest of the crowd was avoiding conversation because of his tortuous speech affliction. Old good-hearted Babbie had to take pity on the lad, and, inserting both feet in my mouth, born out of desperation, I groped about and came up with those words:

"All my life I've wanted an Afghan."

The following morning I was dismayed to find the youth on my doorstep, eagerly asking me to go for a Sunday drive. Stifling an urge to tell him to go put some pebbles in his mouth, I took two aspirin and agreed.

A glorious October day, an open car, and since it took him twice as long as normal to say anything, conversation was minimal, altogether a not unpleasant ride.

"Good God, he's taking me home to Mother."

A terrifying thought that jolted me out of my lethargy as he brought the car to a stop in Darien, Connecticut. There was a charming lady at the door to greet us, but it was obvious that she and George (young man) were not old buddies, and I was baffled. Unbaffling time came when she ushered us into a sunroom in the middle of which was a whelping box that was fighting a losing battle trying to contain a gaggle of two-month-old puppies.

Assuming that he had remembered my dumb remark about my lifelong inhibition, I thought, "How dear of him, he's brought me to see some Afghan pups."

Appropriate puppy noises were in order and I complied, thinking, "No way can these rats turn into the glory of an Afghan. I'll just bet they aren't purebred." The thought had no sooner occurred than into the room bounded gloriousness in gold. Only when our hostess called him "Rudiki" did I realize where I was. This was Marion Florsheim and the famous Rudiki of Prides Hill, of whom even I in my abysmal ignorance had heard.

Intl/Am Ch. Rudiki of Prides Hill and his mistress, the great aviatrix Marion Florsheim.

If you think I was startled before, you should have seen me when Old Lonesome George said, "Which one do you want?"

For once, I was speechless. When I did uncurl my tongue, I stammered enough to make George sound like Laurence Olivier. I fumbled around such protests as "We only met last night over a beer" and "I can't accept this extravagant gift."

George let me un-fluster and then said in one straight line, very quietly, "I've just inherited seven million dollars, and you were kind to me last night."

Ch. Rudiki of Prides Hill. *Photo courtesy Sighthound Review/Bo Bengtson*

"I'll take that one."

(An aside, how is it that guys who inherit seven million dollars shower Cadillacs, diamonds and trips to Montego Bay on girls who are kind to them? With me it's always been dogs, cats, a goat and a trained raccoon.)

So began the saga of ben ghaZi.

Shortly thereafter a temporary reconciliation was affected and my 3-year-old daughter Pat, Punk (puppy) and I went to join my husband in California. We lived on Malibu Beach, and life was bliss for a small girl and a young pup. They ran and swam and lived.

Then came the inevitable, a day that shall go down in infamy. It was a Sunday and I curled up with the *Los Angeles Times*, happy as a pig in the sunshine, when the words leaped out and bit me … "Dog Show."

I had a dog, the dog was registered, and of course he must go to a dog show. Why not? Ask me today and I can give you a hundred reasons why not, but at that time it seemed appropriate. My parents had showed dogs, so this was old stuff. It took a few trips through the yellow pages and some tolerant kennel owners to uncover the mechanics of entering. This done, we waited for the day in smug anticipation.

No one had ever told Punk that Afghans were supposed to grow hair, so he never bothered with it. Life on the beach had raised havoc with what coat he did have, but he was wonderfully muscled and radiantly healthy.

In the wee hours the morning of the show, I whistled Punk in off the beach, combed the seaweed out of his hair, dashed some cologne on him to disguise the smell of the dead seagull he'd rolled in, and we agreed he looked pretty good. His lead was nowhere to be found, an unimportant detail – a bit of clothesline was perfectly adequate, and off we went on what proved to be the road with no return.

If memory serves, we arrived in time to help erect the tents, and someone, possibly the night watchman, pointed out the benches. After securing Punk by his clothesline, we settled back and waited for the glories to roll in.

About nine the other exhibits began to arrive, and our complacency waned. Nowhere was there the slightest resemblance between Punk and the luxuriously coated, stylish dogs parading before our awed eyes. It wasn't long before it was a dread certainty that not only was a ribbon an impossible dream, but unless we moved fast we could expect to be tossed bodily out of the arena.

We lined up in front of the wretched dog on the bench, praying that no one would see him, waiting for a chance to sneak out. We chose a moment when the other exhibitors were gabbing in what to us was a foreign language, to race to the nearest exit. Our hopes for escape were dashed. Standing in front of the door was a pride of fierce and terribly important grandees who thundered, "You can't leave until three o'clock." Back we slunk in total misery.

The dread hour arrived, and Afghans were called. Surrounding Punk as best we could, we marched defiantly to the ring. Since my husband was bigger than I, he won, and I got to show the dog.

There were a couple of classes before us, and I tried a crash course on procedure. At least I went in the right direction, even if I did bump into the lady in front of us. How was I to know when to stop? Cannily placing myself at the end of the line to buy time for observation, I tried to do what the others were doing, but somehow it didn't work for me. Punk had been fairly tolerant until I tried to unscrew his feet and replace them the way I saw it being done. They looked OK to me, but everyone seemed to be doing a lot of fiddling, so I fiddled.

His patience finally gave out when I started the "Picking dog up and dropping front" number. I didn't know what that was supposed to do, but if that's what they

Five Mile's Punjab Ben Ghazi, also known as "Punk."

wanted, I'd go along with it.

That did it. Punk glared at me and quite audibly said, "To hell with this" and went limp. Sweat streaming down my face, I'd managed to elevate the rear, and like a Bassett Hound everything would run to the front and down he'd go, putting the whole frustrating business in reverse when I'd try to set up the front. By the time the judge got to us, I was in tears, but Punk elected to stand still and investigate the nice man who apparently wanted to talk to him.

So harassed was I that nothing but escape was tenable, and I failed to watch what went on when the dogs were moved individually. Thus when my turn came and the judge said, "Please move your dog," I grabbed Punk up in my arms and burst out defensively, "Where do you want me to put him?"

After hours, or so it seemed, of stark humiliation, I was thunderstruck when the judge handed me a blue ribbon. When it penetrated that he meant it for me, I snatched it from his hand and fled. As we passed the family, I yelled, "He's made a mistake. Let's go before he realizes."

My sprint was halted by a kindly soul who blocked my way to explain that we would have to go back. This was inexplicable. We'd won the blue ribbon, what else was there? Besides, I was afraid to go back for fear he'd take it away from me.

You can guess the rest: After further examination and lots of tearing about, that sainted man bestowed upon us a purple ribbon. I had no idea of what that was for until someone explained that we had won five points.

"Where do I go to collect them?"

Do you believe I really said it?

Once again, I was shoved back. This time the ribbon was blue and white.

I forgot to mention all the lovely silver we garnered. None of us had the foggiest idea of what it was all about, but it was clearly a triumph and so nice of that man.

Lawdy me, California hadn't seen such hoopla since Shirley Temple hit. A star was born, that is, until the next show, where we didn't get a ribbon.

That nice man who awarded Punk his first points was Dr. William Ivens, with whom I subsequently became good friends. Until the last time I saw him, he teased me about my clothesline debut.

Punk's show career was hardly stellar. He did finish his championship. Not too handily, I may add, due to his disregard of hirsute desirability. It was as a stud that he proved his mettle. He sired a whole passel of champions, among them my beloved Karli, who is invariably named among the all-time greats.

It was at this, my first show, that a conviction that has never altered was born in me that fine feathers do not a good dog make. As a breeder of some renown and a multi-breed judge, my life in dogs has stretched out over more years than I care to contemplate. How many lives have been affected by that one corner I took. What if I hadn't gone to the movies that night, or felt compassion for that affected boy, or read the *L.A. Times*?

Chapter 2

Chaff Amid the Wheat

"She certainly favors her mother's side."

"Did you ever? Uncanny! The Hepplewhite eyes and chin, exact!"

Fatuous observations like these spread a constant frost on hospital nursery windows, as masked and sterile ladies obligingly display to each nose-pressing relative the newborn fruit of their loin or grandloin.

The dialogue may take a downward turn when both sides of the family coincide their visits. Things may become a might acid, and tend to go like this:

"Do you really think so? Well, at least she doesn't have the Hepplewhite legs."

To an objective observer, there is a distinct possibility that soon there may be more blood on that floor than in the O.R.

On three occasions, I have been awakened in a hospital by someone thrusting into my reluctant arms a large, vocal and crimson chunk of quivering rage who hated me on sight. None bore any resemblance to a human; wild horses couldn't have made me admit a relationship between myself or my husband to this bellicose atrocity. Each time the possibility occurred that they had tossed out the baby and kept the afterbirth. There is a preservative mechanism that instills an almost immediate tolerance, and ultimately affection, but to me at least, it was never first-sight love.

Aside from the disastrous introductions to my own get, the most searing trauma into which I have been plunged has to be the sight of a batch of newborn puppies

I can't say much about what a Brussels Griffon looks like climbing out of the sac, but I can tell you that nowhere, no how, is there anything to touch a newborn Afghan for downright ugly!

ben ghaZi puppies Sinceri, Karli, Punjur, Kurki and Kujer (lying down)

With each litter there is guilt for having perpetrated this cove of obscenities, accompanied by a prayer that they will miraculously disappear or, more wondrously, spring up in the image of glory that was their ancestry.

The doubt of legitimacy festers with the probability of her managing to tryst with the lecherous German Shepherd who had been hanging over the fence and beckoning.

It matters not how often the miracle of multi-birth occurs; the bone-shattering jolt takes place once the mother is at peace, proudly displaying her hideous pile of worms, and smugly expecting accolades.

Time was, ben ghaZi, like most Afghan kennels of the day, rarely sported any colors but the creams and red and mandatory black masks. No one would consider buying anything but those colors, and besides, they won a lot. The explosion on the scene of the immortal Shirkhan of Grandeur changed many minds, and we cast off tradition and bred a lovely cream Karli daughter to him. He himself was dark blue, now most desirable, but in that era considered with much disfavor.

Having to undergo a Caesarian section, Alsi was still anesthetized when we retrieved her from the vet. Gently we placed her and her seven dusky atrocities into the whelping box and sat back, eagerly anticipating the moment of joyous fulfillment when she would open her eyes to behold the heaven-sent little bundles of love. After what seemed a decade, her eyes fluttered. Seeing me first, she softly wagged her tail to assure me that all was in order. All was in order all right, until the startling realization came that she was not alone in her box. Struggling to her elbows to investigate, her reaction was hardly one of gratified maternity. She stared incredulously at her brood for several minutes, and then recoiled in horrified repugnance.

In mighty dudgeon, she leaped from her bed and stalked over to me. Staring me straight in my eyes, she spat out: "What in the hell are those? I thought I was going to the vet's to have my teeth cleaned!" To the day of the departure of the last of those foreign-colored kids, she resented their advances, claiming they weren't hers, she'd never even known anyone that color, and never missing the opportunity to bite any so bold as to approach her.

I mean, if Alsi didn't know what they were, I wish some of these self-styled experts would tell me how they do it. We've all witnessed the scene of the big authority pouncing on a litter barely born, to drag out one squirming, shriveled mouse after another. Bearing them aloft by head and tail, midsection adroop, and pronouncing in unequivocal terms a lengthy critique on each. There are authoritative prognostications of the show career of each, even advice as to which judges to show under. It strikes one dumb with awe!

Many years ago, when my mother and I decided to set the world ablaze by becoming breeders, we went about it in what to us, in our sublime ignorance, seemed the most logical fashion. We introduced a little girl dog to a little boy dog and left the rest to nature.

Sixty days later, ben ghaZi was launched in the form of nine black-masked red puppies. Ten days after that, we were honored by a visit of an exalted breeder who had kindly volunteered her services to evaluate the litter. Ushered into the nursery, she hesitated only for a minute, then pounced gleefully on the poor startled mother and children. One by one she grasped each pup, twisted it into the dangling position, belly hanging perilously from her fingers, and graded each one, for all the world like eggs. Mother and I were so impressed with this volume of knowledge that we never considered questioning her accuracy.

Ch. Karli ben ghaZi, much later in life.

When the time came, we attempted to sell them as she directed, "By dealing them off the bottom." Providentially, neither of us was a "get them while they are hot" salesman, and so it was with the rest sold, there remained the male whom our erudite friend had advised us to rid ourselves of before anyone could see him. We never did manage to palm him off as a pet, and were "stuck" with Ch. Karli ben ghaZi, twice winner of the national specialty and sundry other goodies.

The thought has since crossed my mind that maybe she really did know what she was doing!

As a former breeder of some acceptance, and certainly seniority, I offer my own applied and frequently successful theory on puppy priority. Profit by it, discard it as you will, here it is:

At birth it is questionable if they are mammals of any recognized species. When six weeks have trudged by, I am willing to concede the probability of them being puppies. It isn't until they are at least three months that they get my sanction as to being purebred.

When bewildered owners of a new litter seek my opinion about which puppies can be considered show prospects, I suggest they bring them to me at two years of age. I am pretty astute about recognizing show potential by then.

Apart from my admitted inability to dig among chaff and come up with wheat, there is in me a strong conviction that, appearances to the contrary, I am not God and have no right to take a life, especially one for which I am responsible. There are many people with persuasive, realistic arguments to the contrary who claim that it is a breeder's duty to "cull." To me, "cull," like "put to sleep" or "put down," is a euphemism for "kill." I'd sooner argue with the Ku Klux Klan about running Mohammed Ali for president than dispute another's prerogatives in the disposition of what they consider excess stock – when there they are with triumphant show careers and financial gain to hit me with.

One small for instance on my side is the tale of a puppy bitch who, due to a uterine infection in her mother, was born with a shriveled front leg. Using the oven as an incubator, we kept her alive. The meals around here weren't too good, but Daisy lived and prospered. She was bred once and delivered a beautiful litter. Due to her shriveled front leg, her rear ones were so developed that child bearing was a snap. Ben ghaZi's Desiree is to be found in the background of many of today's Afghans. She could run faster and get into more trouble than anyone I ever met. Her attitude to the others was always a bit condescending about their stupid straight legs, when she had one with a fetching curl. The other dogs spoiled her unbearable. People on meeting Daisy chided us, "Oh, why don't you put that poor thing down?" With which she'd steal their lunch.

She died at seventeen!

Reigh Abram, famous for her Duriegh Kennel, low boiling point and sharp wit (not necessarily in that order), once sat quietly through a lengthy treatise by a lady expounding her expertise in puppy picking. Knowing Reigh, my apprehension mounted as her uncharacteristic silence became more ominous. Ultimately, running out of steam, the authority ended her lecture with "The best time to pick them is when they are wet!"

From Reigh came the zapper … "OK, what color are their eyes?"

Chapter 3

The Gentle Art of Listening

It was probably Oscar Wilde – it usually was – who said, "Ninety percent of a great wit is a good memory." OK, Oscar old boy, wrap your ears around this one: "Sixty percent of a great conversationalist is a good listener." I don't know what wag said that, but as this is my column, I'll take the credit.

My absolutely scandalous delight in analogy sometimes leads me to the precipice of obscurity, and this one is a squeaker. Bear with me, and I'll find the right parable.

From one who has been known to stop dead in the middle of the ring when showing a dog to holler, "I'm a grandmother. I quit!" a lesson in handling may seem a trifle presumptuous. I doubt if Oscar Wilde originated this, but "Don't do as I do, do as I say."

You professionals and semi-professionals, go turn the stove down; I'm not talking to you. Gather round, ye aspirants to recognition. Mother has a few words of admonishment to cheer you on your way. The subject for this month's lecture is "The Gentle Art of Listening." The theme is, learn to listen. I repeat at dictation speed: *Learn to listen!*

Why is it that scores of you with hearing so acute you can detect the sound of a cat walking across a feather mattress in the house next door are afflicted with instant deafness when addressed in the ring by a judge?

Each judge has his own preference for gaiting dogs, and even if you have worn ridges in the backyard practicing the T and he wants an L, you'd better give it to him. It's his bat, so you have to play his ball game. If you don't, he may become irritated, and since you have gone to considerable trouble to be there, the last thing you want to do is irritate the judge.

Unless the conformation of the ring makes it awkward, I myself prefer the triangle. There are circles in which I have been credited with inventing it, but be that as it may, I feel that this is the only way to see a dog's action from the rear, the side and the front, which, when smoothly executed, is accomplished without breaking stride. More about the variations conceived by some later. One of the joys of the triangle is the simplicity with which it can be explained. The word triangle is self-explanatory. You go to that corner, cross the ring to the next corner and straight back to the judge. A piece of cake. No? No! Let me set the scene.

It is eight a.m. on a lovely June morning. We have dispensed with the scratchy recording of the national anthem. Rolling up the mental sleeves, we turn to face the first class. Seven little eager faces are lined up besides seven not-so-eager little Golden Retrievers. Everyone ready for his moment in the sun. Around the ring we go, to come to a dead halt upon the completion of one circle. My feeling is that when I want them to stop, I'll say so – until then, keep going.

Individual examination over, we come to the hard part of gaiting. One by one they come timidly forward. It didn't take me long to learn that instructions had better be explicit. So, accompanying the verbal order with hand signals, I request a triangle. A bright smile of reassurance and off we fly in a victorious sweep describing a perfect T. The next may perform an L and so on. Few have listened to directions, although the open mouth and furrowed brow suggest a CIA agent committing to memory a top-priority classified order. If, in my opinion, the quality of the dog warrants it, I will sometimes reiterate my orders and suggest they try it my way.

Each exhibitor is concerned with himself and his dog and their few minutes in the ring. How many ever consider the fact that by 1 p.m. the judge may have been standing there for four to five hours and repeated this performance a hundred or more times? I keep telling you, but you don't believe me: *Judges are human!* Their feet hurt and their throats get sore from repetition and they want their lunch just like anyone else. So if after their orders have been ignored consistently, they might get a little testy – you try it.

The battle cry of the novice and the experienced buck passer is, "He (she) always puts up handlers or VIPs." As the self-appointed champion of "the little people," I'll go along with that to a degree. I have seen some judges whose record of awarding these golden folk goes beyond the realm of coincidence, and I've decided this publicly.

There are many fine, dedicated people whose past performances glitter with unknown dogs and handlers when their patch to stardom was begun with a helping hand over the swamp of obscurity, proffered fearlessly by a good judge who acknowledges that tomorrow's star is yesterday's Jamoka.

I am not going to launch on a lengthy treatise about why handlers and semi-handlers win so much. Just forget all preconceptions and consider this one small factor of an old theme. The following is based on actual facts. Names have been omitted to protect the innocent (me).

In a class of four there are two representative dogs of approximately equal quality. One is handled by an experienced exhibitor, the other by a familiar type: he who is so snugly wrapped in a cloak of insularity that he is aware of nothing but his dog and himself. The judge has suffered through two lesser dogs and lesser handlers who have ignored instructions and taken off in an elaborate pattern of their own design. As the person in front completes his turn, he proceeds without any ado to move his dog in the desired fashion. Next comes "Old Lonesome George," who marches up to the judge and inquires what is expected of him. Wearily recounting his orders, the judge cannot help a twinge of aggravation as "George" proceeds to do his own thing.

I'm not suggesting that expertise alone is going to net you the full hand of bananas, but, dammit, there has to be a slight psychological edge in the almost gratitude the judge feels. Now –

Oh, this is fun.

While we are contemplating different tastes, I have already described the triangle and why I prefer it. The T to me defeats its purpose, involving as it does much changing of hands and the inevitability of a point where the dog is on the right side of the handler, which confuses both. I guess my bitterness stems from my owner-handler days, when this formation included a frantic vault over my dog and landing splat, a lot of times in the mud.

So if I didn't conceive the triangle, I think I did and don't disillusion me. On the drawing board it is the simplest. However, in the hands of some, it becomes a *pas de deux*. I believe I said that properly executed it is accomplished with a minimum of effort, allowing a back, side and front view of the dog in action without breaking his gait. This, at any rate, is the theory. What happens more often than not is a choreographed maneuver that would do Gower Champion proud.

Babbie and Bob Tongren, 1978.

Here's the way it goes:

Standing in the center of the leading edge of the ring, I call out the first in line and indicate what is desired. If this one is literate enough to understand triangle, it is thusly undertaken. A bright smile, a knowing nod and the dog is rewarded with a thumping whack on his ribs. This is supposed to convey to him that he is to throw up his head, loft his tail and sail around the ring. If the poor beast has sufficient stamina to withstand the bruised ribs, he'll try. Arrival at first base is the cue for a graceful pirouette, and the dog is dragged around behind this charming if irrelevant step. Watch it, Dipthong, here comes another belt on the chest. Across the ring, a final twirl and swat for Dipthong, who by now is gagging and trying to catch his breath. He wonders what he did to deserve that.

I believe that any dog with the good sense to bite the hand that pounds him should automatically win.

Attractive as this terpsichorean presentation is, there is very little "uninterrupted gait." Just a dog with one flat side.

Whereas having my instructions ignored is exasperating, being regarded as a myopic fool is infuriating. Here, laid out in bold, naked words, is one thing that reduces me to a quivering mass of pulsating rage.

For those whose foot this shoe fits, I think it is safe to assume that I am not alone in resenting the apparent assumption that I am an intruder taking money under false pretenses. Who without the guiding hand of the exhibitor would never find a nice head or a level topline. Woe betide the handler in my ring who, having crammed his dog into position, spends the ensuing time delicately running his finger across the backskull, illustrating the perfect head that I would otherwise overlook. So, this one's head isn't so great, but did you ever see the likes of this topline? This is demonstrated by a metronome-like stroking of the back from the neck to the stern.

I always pity the dog without much but the straight front. This pathetic thing is subject to teeth-jarring jolts as the handler places his hand under the chest and elevates him high off the floor, releasing him with such a thud that I sometimes wonder what keeps the shoulder blades from piercing the skin.

There are countless atrocious tricks calculated to educate us judges. There's the one where you hold the dog's muzzle and slowly shake him back and forth. Which only proves that a dog can wobble when manually wobbled. Another old favorite is the pounding on the rear of the stacked dog. As this is invariably accompanied by a triumphant smile, it must prove some anatomical superiority. Just what, escapes me, unless it shows that the dog is pretty good at bracing himself.

Panic always strikes me when I am confronted with a "neck stretcher." If Dipthong hadn't been born with a long neck, this handler is going to see that he gets one before he retires. There are some so grimly determined to improve the creator's work that they all but put their foot on the chest and yank. I am always listening for the preliminary sucking sound as the head flies off in his hands.

There is a hypnotic stare affixed on the unworthy ribbon bestower, calculated to shape you up if the hand signals fail. I usually explain to the eager instructor that I am paid to find these merits and please allow me to muddle through unaided.

Anyway, these are a few of the blatantly insulting things people do under the mistaken guise of "good handling."

I suppose everyone has his own private irritants. My husband's is chewing gum. Normally a fairly even-tempered man, an exhibitor chewing gum in his ring gives him fits. This fact about him has become so well known that one experienced exhibitor sized up another as the potential competition and then offered her a stick of gum.

I have always found baiting unattractive. Not for the purist objections usually raised, but simply if I am trying to see a dog's head and expression, I am not interested in the back of someone's hairy hand as he feeds his dog. The dog's attention is riveted on the liver, which he is allowed to nibble, resulting in curled-back lips, a distorted foreface and liver-covered teeth. The expression becomes one of wild-eyed greed.

There are judges, and God bless them, who are offended by inappropriate garb. I remember years ago, Mrs. Sherman Hoyt dismissing one exhibitor who should have known better for showing in her bare feet. I was told another judge sent a young woman from the ring for sporting a T-shirt decorated with an obscenity.

We wonder why we are not afforded the serious attention given to other sports by the media. Well, look around at some of the ludicrous sights. One of the most common is unfortunately shaped women in pants that make you wonder how they ever got them on. A friend and I were watching some judging last Sunday and marveled at one woman who would have looked less offensive had she been naked. We decided that by mistake she got hold of her daughter's size-10 outfit and, making the best of things, had crammed her size-40 self into it.

As my mother once said to me, "The dog looks great, now suppose you go to the ladies room."

Accolades for the new ruling against hair sprays and bottles of whatever elixir in the ring. If sternly enforced, it has to serve the betterment of purebred dogs. I for one find it enthralling to at last see what some Poodles that I have been interested in really look like. What I'm leading up to is this … I'd like to see all grooming in the ring discouraged.

I am sick and tired of fighting to catch a glimpse of a dog I am there to judge. Lined up in a row for examination, the eye beholds nothing more enlightening than a line of people's behinds as they bend or squat over their dogs, brushing like egg beaters. My feelings about the over-emphasis on coat today are well known, so I won't get into that, but, really, what purpose is served when the dog is standing around all miserably bunched together while his hair-obsessed owner, oblivious to all else, is frantically attacking each lock.

I am cognizant of the tension release that this affords, but holy smoke. If your tension needs relaxing, go punch your mother-in-law, but leave the dog alone.

Chapter 4

Whatever Happened to Trust?

This poignant query was put to me by an old friend who was once active in our world of dogs. He had temporarily receded to give his full attention to the most demanding of educational pursuits, attending law school. Having dispatched the preliminary needs, he has now passed his bar exams and has become a valued addition to a large, prestigious law firm.

He is the gentlest of men whose dogs suffered no worse fate than the most appalling spoiling. He showed a lot and even went Best in Show. We were close friends, staying in each other's homes when geographically feasible. He was much treasured as a friend, and we were elated when he came in a position to resume his dog career and time was no longer an impossible element. He intends to engage the best professional handler possible; however, as members of his family the dogs will be delivered at the shows, rather than be away from home.

My purpose in presenting these extensive credentials is to draw a profile of someone whom any breeder would be enchanted to call a client. Many years ago he had dogs of our breeding and the association became a lasting friendship. No dogs ever had happier lives.

When he felt that the time for re-entry to the arena came, he contacted me and I suggested several people who had puppies of similar breeding to those of his heart (and, I may add, mine). He wasted no time in following my references and shortly did purchase a pretty bitch pup. I guess his memory of Afghan temperament had mellowed so that he forgot the hazards and so proceeded to pamper her to the point that, in his words, "She stands around the house looking gorgeous, but sees no sense in shows." We all know how any Afghan can react to spoiling. Give them their own way once and from then on it's Sulk City. To quote him on a venture to a match show, this coddled wretch turned to him and remarked quite rudely, "Look, Jerko, I don't want to be here, so I'll just hold my breath until I turn blue." So beguiled was he that he fatuously forgot the fact that this willful brat was blue to start with.

We've all been victim to the Afghan's facility to bring us to our knees, and with no further argument my friend set out to buy another, vowing this time to use a common-sense approach. Though the newest acquisition will be a loved house pet, it will be obliged to recognize the rights of others. My friend hoped somewhat wistfully that Baby Dumpling might come unglued when kennel mate and owner would leave for shows, leaving her to tend the house. Such was his intent when he contacted the next on his list of obtainable puppies.

Now … We are caught up on background. OK?

In return to my friend's (I am tired of that – let's call him Steve) inquiry, he received a formal contract. Before I bring a lot of wrath on my head, I am all too aware that times have changed since my breeder days and that crime, corruption and deceit are rampant and that some sort of order is called for, but there must be room for faith and kindness and good manners somewhere. Where better than in a mutual love of dogs?

The contract is lengthy and full of writs and habeas corpuses and all that legal stuff. It is also totally futile! Even my limited legal knowledge can see that this wordy document would hold less water than a kitchen strainer, were contention ever to arise. All it serves is to discourage a potential buyer. Remember, the recipient of this flapdoodle is not only an anxious customer but a lawyer, whose reaction was, "A monument of inefficiency – who needs the aggravation?"

Caveat emptor … let the buyer beware! This is a total summation of this contract. I realize that the breeder in all good faith is attempting to protect his puppies, but there is no consideration for the buyer or even the pup itself, whose transfer becomes as personal as buying a length of stove pipe.

Here are some of the stipulations, as I read them:

1)   The buyer is given five days to determine the usual regard of himself and dog. Now … when I was selling puppies, my feeling was that a dog is not an inanimate object to be bought and returned on a whim. I would tell people, "You can come and visit 30 times if you like. We'll have him checked by a vet. Whatever doubt you may have will be put to rest, *but* once he leaves my house there are no givesy backsyss"! This precluded irresponsible buying.

2)   The buyer is responsible for every aspect of the dog's maturity, physically

and mentally. Remember, we are talking about a baby puppy sold as a show prospect, but in characteristic Afghan indifference to human wants may just decide that dog shows are for dogs, not Afghans. However, beautiful as she may be, the buyer cannot breed her as he chooses without risk of paying an enormous fine.

3)   The buyer doesn't even get to call her his own; a further clause states that these considerable sums are but for a half interest and not until a year has gone by does he get the AKC papers. This is not even in keeping with AKC regulation, which states that the papers go with the dog.

4)   Suppose that Steve, in due time, is offered a once-in-a-lifetime opportunity to practice in, say, Australia, but having owned and loved his pet until maturity, he is loath to put her through the required fifteen months of quarantine. He is still not permitted to surrender ownership to another party, no matter how well qualified they may be. This is couched in such restrictive terms as "never to be sold or given away except to original owner." If he should give or sell his dog, he then forfeits a large sum, and there are no mitigating circumstances suggested. A loving owner may well feel that the interminable quarantine will be far more traumatic for the dog than moving in with an old friend.

Let's go back to the hypothetical, beautiful charmer who loves the master and hates shows. If this is a bitch whose possible championship in this day of formidable competition becomes dubious, she cannot be bred but must be either spayed or returned to the seller. The same contingencies apply to a male, which must be neutered. The seller then offers to replace this one with another in an unspecified future. Anyway, you get the picture.

Being acquainted with both parties, I am saddened. I can understand the seller's motives, which are unquestionably pure. I do suggest that the concept of unrelenting formality is ill advised as well as ineffective. I venture to say that the consummation of this sale would be of infinite gratification to all concerned. I believe that both have the same ideals and strive for mutual goals. I also believe that had a bit more thought and proffered humanity gone into it, each would have benefited and a lasting personal relationship might have been forged. I'll further venture that a profile of either might well fit the other. They are about of an age, both educated, intelligent, thoughtful, kind idealists, but it was doomed before it got on the ground by that damned silly contract.

Let's look at a few of the demands that might well put any thinking person on the trail of another litter.

Babbie as a judge with Reigh Abram of Dureigh fame. The dog is Ch. Winston's Windsong of Dureigh. *Photo courtesy Sighthound Review/Bo Bengtson*

This dog is never to be kenneled but must live in buyer's living quarters. Come on – what happens when Steve in the meantime has bought a male and the day comes when nature's most basic urges start rampaging about? Steve's male and the entire neighborhood of Lotharios start sounding their trumpets of love throughout day and night. Steve is not permitted to secure his own bitch in the safe confines of a boarding kennel for the duration, no matter how well equipped, while he is going about his law business and is loath to leave her unguarded.

Or what if the seller can't fulfill his own contract for any of many reasons? There is no provision for Steve's protection should the seller default by death, disinclination or any of the many vagaries that providence might throw in the path of best intent. The seller agrees to replace the dog with one of a future litter, but even though said in good faith, there is always the possible chance that for any of many reasons there can be no future litters. No thought to that possibility. There is no provision for protecting the buyer.

As Steve said, "Whatever happened to trust? Even the law recognizes that?"

Now, before you jump on my case – I have already admitted that it has been a long time and that trends are different. I am aware that there are unscrupulous people in dogs, but there have always been deceitful, self-seeking people in everything. I just became pretty adroit in sorting them out. It may have been naïve of me, but I patterned my principles upon those of Louis B. Mayer, who said, "If I trust a man well enough to do business with him, then a handshake is all the contract that I want." He was a pretty successful businessman.

In the many years that ben ghaZi was active, I never saw a contract, and with all the puppy sales that went through here there was only one who reneged. My proudest boast has always been that of the true friends that I have today, most are people whom I met when they came to the door to see puppies or who brought bitches to be bred.

I would simply assure people verbally that if they found a puppy to their liking that did not mature to its potential, then I would fill their backyard until one was found that did. There was no question of replacement. This worked just fine!

If a bitch was bred for a fee, it went without saying that a return service was in order, or two, or however many it would take. My only proviso being that the bitch be examined for fertility by a vet after her second miss.

Once the union of pup and owner was declared satisfactory to everyone, I kept no strings … didn't believe in it. I have sold some really nice puppies for little money and there was no formal contract involved. I'd merely specify that at some future date and only if mutually acceptable, I would take a puppy or be free to breed to a male. Even that I would waive if the bitch had less than three pups, and try for future success instead. Perhaps it was the faith that I evinced that made people respond in kind, but it sure worked.

Many of the buyers that I have turned away, who for reasons that I considered valid, were not equipped to cope with the special problems of owning an Afghan. This was based on my faith, in my own discernment, which over the years proved pretty unflagging. I am sure that I made mistakes, but my successes outweighed them and, believe me, they were one and all based on trust.

Chapter 5

The One Single Answer

Bob and I have received an in-depth questionnaire about another breed. This is a well-considered probe into the aspects of that breed that we as judges must emphasize. It is a test of three pages of multiple choice and questions posed in regard to our summation of specific features – movement, head, tail, eyes, condition, etc. – as opposed to whichever aspect in our opinions is of most vital function.

Composed at what has to be considerable expenditure of time, money and energies by one of impeccable sincerity, the questionnaire is to be included in a nationwide survey of all judges approved for that breed and to be published in the magazine dedicated to that breed.

My immediate reaction to any request requiring more thought than a composition of the grocery list is to thrash about and scream in anguish, "Doesn't anybody think that I have nothing better to do? I'm too busy to bother," etc., etc. One would think that Alexander Haig was posed in mid-flight awaiting my verdict on this next move of state. Well, not quite, but old Howard Baker does call now and again.

I was about to toss the whole thing away when the thought struck me of how much of herself this dedicated lady had devoted to her project, and that a civil answer should be forthcoming. At least I hope she considered our reply civil. After an afternoon of discussion, and what for us was considerable analysis, we arrived at the following conclusions.

The variables are too numerous for pragmatic response, I explained to the lady as best I could, so that each question would teem with ambivalence. Using as an example one question about the importance I place on length of neck, I answered, "As an Afghan breeder I may tend to place too much stress on this facet; however,

Babbie and Bob Tongren, 1954. The Afghan Hound is Ch. Karli ben ghaZi; the Boxer, Ch. Birchbark's Gunfire.

one can be faced with a glorious reachy neck but the dog who uses it to separate his body from his head can be totally crippled front or rear, and a compromise must be made." How beautiful if in each class we find one of marvelous type integrating all the parts we deem most worthy of honor; however, rarely is this the case, and again we compromise. Another question asks if at this time we find "higher quality on dogs or in bitches?" Yet another: "What is the most prevalent fault or outstanding virtue?" and "Upon what single feature do you place most emphasis?" It even drags in that old chestnut about type vs. soundness.

My reason for including all of this here is that this questionnaire is so reminiscent of others that we as judges are posed, both written and verbally, and to which I think I have finally found the answer. After some pretty heavy soul-searching and mental acrobatics I present my rather startling conclusion. To our mutual astonishment we decided unequivocally on the single, driving purpose behind the financial ruin, the exhaustion of energy, the breaking labor and the scorching frustration that keeps breeders breeding; the fascinating searching, and contradiction of preconceived conceptions, the abuse, the lies and the misconstruction of our motives that as judges we endure. The one single answer to the whole muddled world of dogs that occupies too much of our time and thought is that ... there is no answer!

There is no generalization that can't be contradicted; there is ambiguity in every answer. Take "How much emphasis do you put on head?" My answer: "An enormous amount, head is where type is, where you tell one breed from another (and here comes the Catch 22) IF the dog wearing the beautiful head is sound enough to make his way across the ring unaided." "How important to you is temperament?" Answer: "Very; however, I will honor a dog of true type displaying a degree of diffidence over an unattractive tail-wagger of no definable type."

These blanket questions and answers must further be broken down into degree. When does diffident become spooky? How prevalent is this failing, and to what extent as judges is it incumbent to recognize and penalize it? Can we as judges be permitted to recognize faulty trends and consider them in our judgment, or must we as judges remain totally objective, ignoring trends that threaten the future of our breed? Speaking for myself I can't, and I find that I am apt to tolerate a feature that I might have frowned on at an earlier time, in favor of one that appears to be riding a tide of popularity, but one whose perpetuation may well endanger my concept of breed type.

As judges we are sometimes accused of being inconsistent. I prefer the term elastic. What might have been a profound conviction five years ago may have been altered by a fashionable whim that I feel is threatening, or my own priorities may change. To go back to Adlai Stevenson, "My most cherished prerogative is the right to change my mind."

There are variables within variables within variables. Traveling from one end of the country to the other we see this manifested. We live in a very large country; the flora and fauna indigenous to one area is vastly altered or even non-existent in another. The variance carries over into dogs, either due to proximity of one breeder to another, or due to the reluctance to ship bitches for either humane or financial reason, and can make a profound difference in type.

Climate can change the manner in which puppies are raised; access to outdoor, year-round living can stimulate appetite and encourage exercise, perhaps inducing growth. Factors made impossible by life in colder climates where exposure to the great outdoors is by dint of necessity limited, but conversely throwing dogs and humans together more in a mutual war against cold, in turn socializing the pup.

Even economic conditions may exert an influence. In financially distressed areas, people may find it impossible to indulge in some of the desirable goodies when inflationary prices put them out of reach; then puppies and children, by force, make do. This came to mind when I saw cottage cheese, once considered essential to puppy rearing, priced at $2.49 per container.

Further variables: In most sections there is a core of similar type and a periphery that is recognizably influenced by far-flung brethren. Some areas seem to be completely isolated from the rest of the world, and nothing but a native blossom is to be tolerated or ever acknowledged.

Just recently I saw a remarkable example of area variance. In the span of less than a month, I judged Afghans in two far-flung states. In the first of these shows, I was hard pressed to ferret out enough merit to fill the placements. Happily, there were several that could win anywhere, but the overall entry was sorry indeed … in my opinion.

I have long felt and probably been guilty of outrageous indiscretion by publicly stating that the best general concentration of Afghans is to be found in the middle part of the country. I am not going to keep repeating "in my opinion." Clearly it is "my opinion," or I wouldn't be filling up these pages with it … so, right or wrong, agree or disagree, keep remembering this is one woman's opinion.

The second show of which I speak was a sizable entry in Columbus, Ohio. I was both thrilled and sorrowed by the marvelous quality of the majority of dogs that poured into my ring.

Thrilled, because my faith in the future of the breed was renewed, and sorrowed because I had to deny ribbons to many dogs that at some shows I'd have placed in Groups. Selection was reduced to nitpicking. I was forced to make decisions on relative detail. Our governing body demands that we remain non-committal, but how often I wanted to run after an exhibitor and explain that his dog lost because

I only had four ribbons and my decisions were based on what well might have been either temporary or miniscule factors. To the best of my knowledge, most were amateur handled. I saw no jostling for position, no exaggeration in stacking and little evidence of artifice in grooming; although each dog was clean and well put down, there wasn't a clipper mark anywhere.

As an aside, I was delighted with the physical layout of my ring. Mine was of adequate size to accommodate the well-represented Open classes, and, best of all, there were *no mats*. Obviously, on slippery flooring some sort of traction has to be provided, but this was in a fairground building, and the floor was rough cement. By omitting boundaries that mats demand, the judge is free to move the dogs to their best advantage. I loved being able to have each one circle individually with no danger of tripping, and there was great psychological freedom in the large, unguided space.

It is my fondest wish that people could retain their objectivity and apply it to dogs. If they could understand that a conscientious, able judge is doing the best he can, that because a dog lost, it needn't imply political intent, that rejecting a friend can hurt and that on a different day those decisions can be reversed. They are made within a frame of the two minutes allotted to each, which is in fact insufficient for a big class, and I for one have suffered many second thoughts and self-reproach. But until someone comes up with a better plan, we have to do the best we can with it.

Undoubtedly, every judge alive has at one time or other become the target of hate letters. Often they are anonymous, and these get the treatment they deserve, a fast trip to the waste basket. Although the AKC asks that we turn the signed ones over to them, I usually reply myself.

Of all the vicious attacks I have had made on me, the vilest came after the Columbus show, and sadly from one whom I had once thought of as a friend. What is it about the supposed sport of showing dogs that brings people to the depths of perfidy? People who would never be rude to a stranger will willingly and with the forethought required to write a letter revile and debase someone for whom they had once professed affection.

Funny part is, he wasn't even there.

Chapter 6

Nothing Succeeds Like Excess

"Nothing succeeds like excess!"

An aphorism that may well have been coined by some soulless officiary whose words dictate dog-show victory. The beauty-pageant syndrome from which our top-winning show dogs suffer is analogous to many breeds, especially the coated varieties. "Overdone" is a succinct if harsh term, and it is applicable to most of our feathered friends. Based on the old principle that if one is good, two is better, we have the snowballing effect of the bigger the better.

Nowhere is this truism more tenaciously glued to triumph than in the presentation, for want of a better word, of the Afghan Hound.

Fret not yourself. I am not about to launch another Babbie attack into the horrors of hirsute redundancy, nor on the giant proportions of some. I won't even mention the improbable acrobatics involved in stacking. Rather, I aim to answer the piteous lament of judges and their rapidly proliferating claim of impotence to adjust awards to meet the standard.

I am so tired of hearing "Everyone trims, so what can I do about it?" or "Only the novice will be penalized, as the pros do it so well as to be undetectable," or "Trimming and stripping is not a disqualification." Judges feel helpless to halt the acceleration of winning dogs that are little else but a tribute to the sculptor's art.

For those too new to be aware, or the many who have forgotten, or the multitude who just don't give a damn about my persuasions, I am going to quote myself. Bear with me. I have a reason for all of this over and above personal regard. I, in fact, have a solution to the judges' dilemma as to what can be done about it, so hang in there.

"I have screamed myself hoarse about stripping and scissoring, am bored to death mentioning it again. It is an exercise in futility. If this is what they want, let them have it, but please don't call them Afghan Hounds. Go ahead, strip saddles to the startlingly precise definition between sides and back. Take away the desired flat desert feet and round out nice, even Setter extremities. Why breed dogs with long necks when a flick of a clipper will carve one to your liking, or worry about saddles when so many are precisely one clipper head wide? The artifice that I find most distasteful is the scissoring of the undercarriage to simulate a tuck-up of loin. While all of these cosmetic atrocities are unforgivable, they are rarely harmful to the dog – but how about poor old Dipthong, who had the bad taste to have lighter than ideal eyes? No problem, a few drops of Belladonna will expand the pupil and obliterate the light eye. Of course the poor dog can't see to walk, but the eyes appear dark."

So, I too have despaired of remedying a situation that spells doom to the breed I love – until I decided to explore the options. To the ubiquitous cry "Trimming is indeed an affront," the black border around the "King of Dogs," I say that there is a very tidy if improbable solution. The Afghan Hound Club of America could amend the standard declaring such artifice a disqualification. However, not known for imagination, innovation or even willingness to recognize the imminent doom of the breed whose preservation it is their sworn duty to protect, it is doubtful that the club would risk popularity by affirmative action.

Should a miracle occur within the confines of that august body making them aware of the potential of constructive force, there is no doubt that such an amendment would be a monument of cautious ambivalence and probably read in very small print: "Disqualification: Excessive trimming." Not unlike the ludicrous "a little pregnant," what is excessive trimming, and who decides? Here is where the artisans triumph, those who can hand-pluck a saddle, neck or shoulder, face or croup in an almost indiscernible way. The key word here is almost. Anyone familiar enough with the breed to warrant judging approval knows full well that no fully coated Afghan of maturity is apt to have a saddle so shiny, or a neck and face like a Cocker. A natural pattern will almost invariably sport a tuft of hair over the croup and the undercarriage we see would do credit to "The Long Grey Line." Any trimming is excessive!

So, let us discard the possibility of decisive action on the part of the parent club and go over their heads to the real governing body, the American Kennel Club, whose book of rules is dominant above all and tells us very clearly in Chapter 15, Section 9: "A dog that is blind, castrated, spayed or which has been changed in appearance by artificial means except as specified in the standard for its breed may not compete at any show and will be disqualified." Now here is the wording direct from the standard of the Afghan Hound under the heading of "Coat": "The Afghan Hound should be shown in its natural state: The coat is not clipped or trimmed." I would love to rest my case here, but, anticipating the inevitable resistance that I will meet, I'll argue my point. Ironically, it was the regular breed column in the *AKC Gazette* that prompted me to examine the question once more and poke about seeking an answer. It is written by the much admired Betty Stites, approved judge and former president of the parent club. In the AKC's very own official organ, Mrs. Stites says:

"The beginning of a New Year would seem to be a fine time to open an old can of worms. All of you out there with tack boxes filled with thinning shears, stripping knives, Oster blades and the rest, who constantly tell me your dogs are as natural and untouched as the day they were born, this is for you!

"Our standard tells us the Afghan Hound should be shown in its natural state, neither stripped nor trimmed. We are all aware that there is very probably not an adult Afghan in the ring with an owner/handler who has attended more than three shows that hasn't had its coat cleaned up a bit. The clamor of voices at ringside grows louder. The AHCA should do something about trimming? The AKC should do something? *Somebody* should do something? My question to you is: *What?* What should be done, who should do it, and how? Trimming is not listed as a disqualification in the Standard. As presented, it is only one of a number of faults. The longtime Afghan owner/handler/exhibitor is so skilled at trimming that it is rarely discovered by the judge. If we, as judges, penalize dogs who are visibly stripped, we are probably penalizing the novice who had botched a job, rather than the true artisan who never lets a clipper mark show. Is that what we want? Do we really want to punish the new and unskilled while the real culprit goes free? If we are to penalize anyone, how is it to be done? This is your forum. Let me hear!"

Before you jump in my face, I am quick to admit that I have never disqualified an Afghan for being trimmed. I tend to make my displeasure known in terms that leave little doubt and make it clear that the dog is being penalized for trimming by being placed lower in his class than he might well have been had the handler not employed the means of apparent artifice, as I am sure do other judges. An amusing aside: I have never, ever gone through this ritual without the handler assuring me that it was not his fault, that the dog had been altered by his wife, kennel help, child or (if a handler) the owner is to blame and always in tones of hushed agreement, that it is a woeful deed indeed.

Babbie judging the Afghan Hound Club of California specialty in Santa Barbara in 1966. First in the Veterans class, far left, was Ch. Shirkhan of Grandeur with Sunny Shay; behind him, his son Ch. Akaba's Top Brass, with Lois Boardman, who was second. Next to him is another Shirkhan son, Ch. Patrician's Sherwood, who was unplaced. The cream dog is Ch. Gandhi of Lakoya, who was third. Far right the fourth-placed Ch. Triumph of Azad. *Photo courtesy Sighthound Review/Bo Bengtson*

Obviously this procedure is inadequate, as exhibitors simply sharpen up their shears, put a new blade in the stripping knife and proceed to a more tolerant judge. No doubt this is a fast trip to the title of Miss Bad Odor Judge of the Year, which keeps a lot of judges from taking a stand. However, *not* taking a stand is cyclical, and so the manufactured little machine is thrust under the benign gaze of he whose choice is the attractive road to popularity and so overlooks that which he knows (if he is able to read) is wrong and thus throws open the door to greater heights. The malfeasance manifested is of course that these sad travesties are imitated by the ambitious newcomer, and so the cycle goes on.

I am not insisting that Mrs. Stites or any other judge open that can of worms. It would veritably be sticking the head in the hornets' nest and the inevitable brouhaha would be embarrassing, frustrating and more than likely self-defeating. It would take a Joan of Arc among judges to initiate this program, and she got the original hot seat for her heroism.

I don't even predict that I, who have been known to trample angels in my rush to tread where they feared to go, am prepared to employ this radical position – but then I don't say that I am not ready, either. I have a glorious list of unfinished business that I am saving for the last show I judge and may add this, but then again I may not wait. I have to consider the possibility that this expedient might hasten my retirement.

Chapter 7

"Free – To Good Home Only . . ."

All of you starry-eyed dreamers out there whose rose-colored glasses are befogged in illusion, give me your hands and let me lead you on the path of reality. For those who think a judge's life is glory, glamour, adulation, riches and trips to Santa Barbara, I'll sing a song of how it really is.

When I read the premium list for one show in Ohio, I smiled beatifically and thought I had finally reached my reward. There were the glowing words, "Judging will be held indoors." My joy was short-lived; I hadn't read the fine print, which said, "Except for Gordon Setters, which will be done outdoors." Guess who was judging Gordon Setters? Eighty-nine big, black-and-tan, wet dogs … in a freezing downpour. There is no way to cope with that many dogs under a tent, so there I was. Which takes me to a peeve. That is the exhibitors who lustily air their grievances against having to show their dogs in the bad weather. For pity's sake, I don't want to hear it. They are out in whatever element is uncomfortable at the time for the brief period their class takes. The judge has to stand out there all day. At that, most judges, concerned for the dogs, will try to keep them under the tent when possible, which usually means that she or he has to place himself outside the edge of the tenting. So enough of your moaning.

Even in the midst of misery, some sun must shine. Here is a true story that I have to share.

At this same Ohio show, I was judging Toys in the morning, naturally indoors and before the rain started. Anyway, apparently a disgruntled Pug exhibitor got in such a flap about the color of his ribbon that he took his gruntles to the show chairman for airing. Their conversation went thus:

Exhibitor: "I want to lodge a protest against Mrs. T."

Chairman: "What is the nature of your complaint?"

Exhibitor: "She wasn't very nice to me."

Chairman: "Did you win?"

Exhibitor: "No."

Chairman: "Did she examine your dog thoroughly?"

Exhibitor: "Well – yes."

Chairman: "Did she move your dog?"

Exhibitor: "Well – yes."

Chairman: "Then why are you complaining?"

Exhibitor: "Well, she just wasn't very nice to me."

Chairman: "That's too bad, but I'll tell you what. There are houses where you will find ladies who will be very nice to you. It will cost more money and you can't take your dog, but they will be very nice to you."

Is that funny or what?

There is very little to be said in favor of viral pneumonia, but like any dark cloud, if you keep turning it over and over you'll find a small silver lining. Feeling too wretched to do anything, there is time to think. Being a scribe of sorts, committed to matters dog, I naturally spend most of my thinking time beating my head about what to say this month, or at least a new approach to a time-worn topic.

The pneumonia caught up with me later leaving Ohio and proceeding to Virginia for a long weekend of more sodden, spiteful, frigid weather. When the last day finally chattered its close, I was in my motel room, gingerly removing dripping layers of nasty clothes to realize that even my underwear was wet, and I had gone through two raincoats! At this point the awful truth was on me. I knew that I was one sick lady. Due to leave for Fairbanks, Alaska, on Thursday, I was loath to tell those nice people that they would have to replace a judge for three groups, so I wrapped my ailment in a layer of false good cheer and took off for what seemed certain doom. Thank the lord, the weather, just eighty miles from the

Arctic Circle, was glorious, seventy-eight degrees and twenty-two hours a day of sunshine. So in spite of my conviction to the contrary, I did live.

While thrashing about on my bed of pain, a succinct thought occurred. Every dog magazine is replete with cogent articles on shows, handlers, judging show dogs and nearly every aspect of our mutual insanity, but very little has been said about the people who buy dogs.

I'm not talking about the long-time fancier who wants to incorporate a new line to infuse fresh blood into his, or the one who elects to try a new breed, or a breeder who sees a particularly arresting specimen and buys it to show. I am talking about the person who has wanted a dog for years and finally decides the time is now. For whatever purpose, to show or simply enjoy the companionship, or even those who feel a particular breed will lend him an aura of status. There are unfortunates who, lacking personal appeal, think a glamour dog like a Poodle or an Afghan will be an assist in attracting attention. A hat-check girl in a New York nightclub told me that she was making a fortune in caring for dogs once a conquest has been consummated. I don't suppose that anyone has to be overly bright to figure that a Great Dane in close quarters will sweep a coffee table clean with his tail, or that a team of bouncing Boxers is not a happy choice for a small child or the elderly or infirm, or that Terriers tend to bark, making enemies of city-dwelling neighbors. Conversely, it is hardly reasonable to ask a Shih Tzu to menacingly prowl the reaches of a large estate and play guard dog.

Of all breeds, none should be sold more selectively or bought more carefully than the Afghan, yet none is more recklessly chosen or sold in a more profligate manner, often with an ignominious end.

Idly scanning the classifieds, this leapt out at me, and against my better judgment, I had to investigate … *Free – To a good home only! Two eight-year-old male Afghan Hounds, excellent disposition, good with children. Call …*

Pretending to be a prospective owner, I called the number. The female voice on the other end reassured me of all good, good qualities of the two dogs and then threw in some additional information. They had pedigrees a mile long, although she couldn't lay her hands on the papers, nor remember any of the names of forebears. She hastened to assure me of the enormous amounts of money to be made on these dogs as studs, or if I cared to purchase a female the puppies would bring thousands of dollars.

Although it broke her heart, she had to get rid of them because her son was no

Babbie's son Guy with "Apryl."

longer interested and she could not take care of them herself. In a somewhat vicious probe, I unearthed that she is not elderly or ailing, nor does she go to work. She bought the dogs as puppies for her son, who had seen a picture of an Afghan and would die unless he owned a pair. The boy at that time was thirteen, so although she loved the dogs, what could she do? I tried to advise her that two eight-year-old Afghans would not be easy to place and asked what her alternatives were ... Must I go on? As much as she would hate doing it, she would have to send them to the pound.

I spent a sleepless night wrestling with my heart, and good sense won out. All of our priorities have changed, and our lives irrevocably altered. We travel constantly, and there is just no place for even one of the breed of my heart ... I didn't make the call.

Were this an isolated case, it would be saddening but bearable, but we all know it's not. I have taken a number of Afghans from the pound and placed them. In fact, the dog warden still calls when he has one in for disposal. I even had a research lab call me once. The lady who heads the lab was a sensitive person who, as she said, "Hated to do this to this lovely dog." I told her to bring him out and I'd see what I could do. This case ended happily; by the time she arrived here she had fallen in love and that lucky dog had a fine home. I don't have to draw word pictures of the ignominy. We've all seen the gross negligence accorded Afghans by people who buy a dog to suit an image but are unwilling to cope with the problems of a glamour dog.

The irresponsible buyer is only superceded by the seller. In a frenzied passion to produce the perfect show dog, breeders faced with a frightening surplus will go to any length to rid themselves of the unwanted encumbents. I heard a well-known breeder, a genius at the hard sell, assure a prospect that "grooming is no problem, run your nails up the dog's back against the lay of the hair, he will then shake and all the mats will fall out." He sold a lot of puppies.

Grooming is but one of the problems. How many people are prepared for the supreme dexterity of an Afghan in sliding out of a three-inch slot and taking off? Or their ability to find burberry bushes and mud puddles to romp in? Do over-eager breeders warn a naïve customer not to expect "Good Old Pal"? The Afghan has yet to be born who yearns to fetch the pipe and slippers; rather, he expects you to get them for him. Does the big hype ever include a dissertation on the joys of tempting an Afghan to eat? Every one I owned would yawn in my face when presented with a meal I'd slaved for hours over. Are they ready to be snubbed, to understand that the best chair is no longer theirs, or that they can never again leave the kitchen without glancing back at the counter, that an Afghan can be eleven feet tall when he wants to steal something?

They don't know what revenge is until they own an Afghan. Apryl once took five of my coats from a closet and destroyed the linings because of an imagined slight … should she choose she would commit a misdemeanor on my side of the bed to keep me in line.

There is a masochistic dedication requisite to owning an Afghan that few, when faced with actuality, are prepared for. That is why we see "Free to a good home only …"

"The puppy in the window" is appeal unparalleled. Even the wary cognoscenti have to fight an impulse when passing a pet shop. What chance does the unenlightened have? Who is to warn him that the wistful baby will become an Old English Sheepdog? This is a breed that has suffered massive disfavor at the hands of TV commercials in which they have achieved a pinnacle of favor. Who is to warn a gullible public that the immaculately groomed and well-behaved specimen on the tube can become an obstreperous, matted nuisance unless great care is taken? The area in which I live is replete with dirty, timid and shaved-down OES, thanks to the proliferation of media push. A few years back, Bassets suffered a similar fate because of Cleo, a TV favorite who did disservice to a nice breed.

If anxious and star-struck purchasers won't look into the future, then breeders must dust off their consciences and consider the fate of that pup that they are so anxious to sell, which just might include an ad in the classified "Free – to a good home only."

Chapter 8

Another Look at the Afghan Hound Standard

Perhaps because in what some might call their dubious wisdom the AKC has approved me for new breeds and rounded out my sanction to judge the whole Toy Group, I find myself regarding the value of standards as a new judge.

Ideologically, a judge is well versed in all aspects of a breed before applying for approval. Ideology is purist but unfeasible. If each judge were an expert in each breed before he applied, the implication is that he has devoted years to learning the whims and idiosyncrasies as well as the basic fundamentals and is able within a two-minute span to assess the relative values of type and structure and in that short time to apply the variables to the age-old question, "Can he do what he was meant to do?"

If each show were to boast this kind of expertise for each breed, there would be precious few with the right to pass on more than a few breeds. Obviously, no one could claim the right to judge Groups or Best in Show. So, concessions must be made and it is up to breed clubs to help judges learn all that is possible. Seminars and slide presentations are fine but often impossible for some to attend. The written word is the most help a judge can have, not by standard alone but a well-thought-out clarification of these standards that a judge can work over and renew in his mind constantly.

Some standards are so explicit and wordy as to be inapplicable to dogs by a judge on a limited schedule. The Great Dane standard has pages of definition and precise measurement. It would take a judge a half-hour to comply with all the requisites. On the other hand, the German Wire Haired Pointer is given 14 short lines and tells just that here is a medium-sized dog with a wire coat.

Some fall in between these extremes, and many are magnificently indecisive.

How about a head that is described as having a "pleasing expression"? Pleasing to whom? A head that pleases a Rottweiler breeder is sure not going to tickle a Borzoi breeder. Another pet peeve is anatomical parts described as "Not too long, not too short." What does that mean? Too long or too short for what?

I have always thought that the Afghan Hound standard is a model of descriptive phrase. Though precise in its mores, it allows flow with the lines of a dog who is a "King of Dogs." The often-mocked phrase "Eyes gazing into the distance as if in memory of ages past" is a jewel of clarity to anyone with any degree of aesthetic perception. It describes a proud aristocrat of fluid grace whose eyes reflect the wisdom of antiquity and whose linear definition sets him apart.

As standards go, I have always felt that this is one of the few that defines to the reader the "feel" of the dog. Well, that is how I feel, but there are too many approved to judge the breed who cannot apply these elegantly lyrical words to the dog. But then I suspect that to these people, art is a Hallmark greeting card.

Some time back I received in the mail a plain manila envelope with the sender unidentified but containing a splendid clarification of the Afghan standard. I hope that whatever it is, it will be made available to all fanciers and judges of the breed.

Written as a dialogue between two voices, it is apparently devised for an educational function of some kind. The manuscript defines the standard in the second voice, and then comes a marvelously comprehensive interpretation by the first. There is so much value in the words that I am going to take the liberty of quoting some of it, and hope that I won't be out of line.

Starting with the head, the first voice emphasizes the chiseling as a hallmark of the breed and, in a precise definition of the ideal, goes on to explain the whys of the importance of the words and explaining how a punishing mouth is vital to a hunting hound.

There is much wordage on the eyes and expression, the first voice explaining why "a Sighthound is farsighted and will pull his head back when focusing on near objects," but in no way advocates this as correct posture.

This very facet of the Sighthound's makeup is in large part responsible for one of today's greatest fallacies. The regrettably straight front assembly that we see so much of is due to a predominance of straight shoulders, which have become so commonplace that they are accepted. In fact, in some dogs this lack of shoulder angulation almost produces ewe necks, resulting in a very stylish head carriage with the head held way back, and in fast action the shoulders will precede the head. This is often admiringly termed "showmanship."

The body of the Afghan is referred to as being composed of sharp angles, as opposed to the rounded curves of most dogs. The topline is called level but broken by prominent hip bones. How often have we heard a dog who boasted hip bones criticized by a judge as being "out of condition"? The typical definitive tracings of the spine are also jumped upon and derided by critics.

Bless my anonymous donor, there is space provided in this fine script for a croup; a most distinguishing feature of the breed, but almost non-existent. The word is unknown in many circles.

A full description of the tail and the variances of each is followed by my favorite line, which says, "nowhere in the standard does it call for the Afghan's tail to be up at any time except when the dog is in motion," which means that the death grip exhibitors have on a tail is an unnatural and undesired artifice. To me, a dog standing with his tail at ease presents a far more dignified figure than one who appears to be held together by a handler propping up each end.

I have long decried the manipulation of handlers in stacking a dog with the hindquarters extended so far behind that it is nothing short of a miracle that the dog can maintain his balance. The hind feet should be placed directly under the dog's tail, not yanked so far out that it has to be torturous. There is a description of the hind legs, calling them "wishbone" in shape, an appearance precluded by exaggerated extension; a practice currently prevailing contrives to make a class of Afghans into grotesque, pitiable caricatures, distorted by handlers and honored by undiscerning judges.

My knowledgeable author includes some weighty words about coat and trimming, which he/she points out is a flagrant violation of the standard, which calls for a natural dog. This is coached so well that I am going to quote directly from the manuscript.

"The Afghan's coat pattern is both his glory and his nemesis. The traditional pattern of a short-haired face, saddle and neck is for a mature hound. At a year many Afghans are fuzzy, gawky teenagers, so over-anxious exhibitors will artfully trim a saddle (neck and underline) for the show ring. An overabundance of coat may not conform naturally to the required pattern and can mask the angular hunter underneath. The standard clearly calls for short hair on the neck and

Patterned dogs in an undated vintage photo. "Patterned" refers to a low saddle or, as pictured here, short hair on the cuffs.

allows for bare pasterns."

This last sentence points out something that has become a major problem in the breed. There are some of us who go so far as to feel that the patterning lends an exotic look and is quite characteristic of the breed. There have been too many times when otherwise beautiful dogs have been severely penalized in the ring for what is natural and attractive. Judges have admitted the superiority of dogs that they have put down for being patterned. Though the standard is quite specific on this point, it is one of many issues that might well benefit by clarification in the form of additional material, such as the Yorkshire Terrier Club and others have put out for a the edification of those judges who may be taking on additional breeds.

The subject of color is well covered. It is my personal feeling that the standard should be changed to eliminate the part that says that white markings are undesirable, or at least be more thinking in the wording. I am sure that many prospective buyers have diligently read the standard and perhaps shied off because of white markings. I have seen very few puppies that didn't have a white chest, toes or a tip on a tail, most of which are blended into the adult coat in time.

On size: "The oversized Afghan can be an insidious evil, as he clearly stands out and impresses. It is up to the judge to train his eye on specimens of proper size so as to recognize those that are too large – or small. Any great size variation must be handled as any other deviation from the standard's requirements."

Our correspondent should be listened to on the topic of temperament, an ever-prevailing problem. It brings tears to my eyes to see my breed cringing in panic at the approach of a stranger. It says, "The aloof Afghan may not make friendly overtures, but it is unacceptable for him to panic or be nasty.

"The Afghan Hound is by tradition and heritage an independent hunter and will make his own friends. He is usually friendly when allowed time to take the measure of visitors, but will not be forced. Once acquainted, he is a true friend. In the show ring he is the epitome of dignity and style, standing and moving."

In essence, the anonymous script says it all. Having batted my head on the stone wall of indifference for many years, it is good to know that someone, somewhere, is joining the fray. I am sure it is an exercise in futility to hope, but I will keep on praying that some of our more thoughtful fanciers may take heed.

Chapter 9

Withholding Judgment

What I'd really like to know is, how come everybody is a judge? If they are all this qualified, how come so few of us wear the purple ribbon?

The most unequivocal pronouncements iterated and reiterated at shows are: "He should have given Winners to the Reserve Dog!" "The Cattle Dog should have won the Group!" "She should have given it to poor Joe after all the troubles he has had." And the one most often heard from the ringside admirals: "She should have withheld the ribbon!"

Sure, she should have, but woe betide the judge who withholds from the astute critic who most frequently mouths off this admonition.

There are as many opinions on this subject as there are judges, the only unanimity being that it should be done more often. Even in agreement of the advisability of this radical system, we are all reluctant to deliver the crushing blow. Perhaps we identify with the crestfallen exhibitor, mindful of our early careers. No one wants to be the villain, an automatic designation when the judge virtually says, "This dog is unworthy." Rare indeed is the exhibitor who can realistically recognize a withheld ribbon as anything other than a personal slur. Our dog is an extension of our own ego, and by saying, "This dog is not worthy," the judge in essence appears to be saying, "You are not worthy."

Odious though the chore is, as judges it is our sworn responsibility to protect the basic precepts of the improvement of purebred dogs, to stem the tide of mediocrity with which shows are flooded, and so we must deny the badge of merit to those who, in our estimation, fall short.

As guilty as most, I have often handed out unwarranted awards, stifling my conscience rather than face the hurt that I must face if I tell the proud owner the awful truth.

There are some to whom rejection is such a personal affront that they will run to the AKC rep with a complaint either wholly fallacious or embroidered out of proportion. The representative in turn must include this in his report, and deservedly or not the unhappy judge comes under fire from the powers that be. It is a shame that those so quick to air their laments don't pause a minute to consider the ramifications.

Babbie showing one of her first generation of home-bred Afghan Hounds, Kujur ben ghaZi, who was whelped in 1950.

What I really want to say to the exhibitor from whom I have withheld first place is this, "This hurts me more than it does you. I absolutely hated doing it, and wish I had been able, in good conscience, to have avoided doing it."

If only exhibitors would understand, and again I say it, that judges are human. We have all been there. I never had a ribbon withheld when I was showing dogs, but the truth may well be that it was more good luck than good management. Most of us have suffered the agonizing chill of the last few minutes when we know the judge is mentally lining up his placements. Believe it or not, most of us sympathize. We only have four ribbons to bestow, and we hope we can hand them all out and keep our integrity intact. Sometimes, however, we cannot – and, honest, guys, it is a trauma for us, too.

This all came to light last week when I was judging in a far remove. It was the end of a very full day, and I was so weary that I thought I might have agreed to anything to finish my assignment without incident and get back to my motel and HBO. Anything, that is, until my last breed for the day – one on which I have my firmest convictions and a seniority that entitles me to them. I don't claim infallibility, simply the right to conviction.

Before my despairing eyes, there filed into my ring a class of four, and the terrible truth was on me. I knew what I had to do. I carefully examined each, hoping against hope that I would find sufficient merit in one to enable me to gracefully depart those alien shores with no enemies made. I felt that it was taking me forever to judge the class of four. The truth was that they had been judged when they arrived and the adjucation that was taking so long was that of self-examination, "Come on, Babbie, you know what you have to do – do it!" Still I fiddled and stalled and hoped that some wonderfulness would leap out at me. Anyway, the long and the short of it was that I mustered my courage and told the dear anxious faced, "I am truly sorry, but I cannot award a first-place ribbon." I handed out second, third and fourth and, though the owner probably didn't recognize it as such, one was lucky enough to leave empty-handed, which, in fact, means that there is no official report of that one being present.

It is a certainty that all of those people were so busy being angry that none noticed that I was blinking back tears. Does that sound overly dramatic? Perhaps, but nonetheless true. It ached for me to do it, knowing full well how much work and time and money had gone into the presentation that day and how terrible is the disappointment.

One of the rejected owners refused to leave the ring, demanding an explanation of my untenable behavior. I explained that if she would wait until I had finished the breed, I would be glad to discuss it with her. Of course I was secretly hoping that she would calm down before the moment of reckoning was due. No such luck! When she did return, it was in absolute fulmination! It was obvious that no amount of reason would placate the lady. I tried to tell her that in actuality I was suggesting that if she wanted to show, it might be wise to get a dog worth showing. She assured me it was because of my longevity in the breed that she had come, and she felt that as she had spent so much effort and time grooming her entry, I owed it to her to award the dog a blue ribbon. To bring me to my knees she also assured me that the dog had won many ribbons. I am sure he has and will win many more, but is that what it is all about, dear lady?

Someone once said, "No one shows for a judge's opinion. They show to win points," and I think in most cases that may be true. Certainly this irate young woman wasn't looking for opinion, and she absolutely hated it when she got it. I have filled pages in every book that will have me on my concept of type. Happily, most people have an idea of my mores and rarely do I see dogs too far afield. It would seem to me that it would behoove people in this day of frightening economy and accelerated pace to avoid a terrible waste of resources and make themselves aware of judges' appetites.

I know that absolute objectivity is asking more than most exhibitors can give, at least at the time when their feelings are wounded and humiliation is rife, but it would be such an advantage to all if once the dust has settled they would take a long, cool look at themselves and their dogs and ask themselves some basic questions …

Is the judge a sub-human who enjoys delivering a stomach punch?

If not, what does she get out of it?

Is my dog perhaps not the type she has owned, bred and advocated?

Will my dog ever finish, and if so will his championship be won under respected judges?

What will it cost, in time, money and peer approval?

Will he ever be a specials dog or just a very expensive champion, and then what?

Is this what I want to breed?

Can I be wrong?

As the unhappy lady left my ring, she flung at me her assurance that I would never see her as an exhibitor again. I truly hope this is not so. I would like to believe that in spite of her momentary fury, perhaps, just perhaps, my drastic action might have given her pause. And if enough judges will have the courage and the true love of the breed to do as I did, she may see her dog as he really is, and avail herself of one that is worthy of her energies.

Withholding ribbons is a miserable, masochistic thing to do, and it is love of good dogs that prompts judges to do it. We know what we are in for when we deny an award, and we dread it. Judging is not a popularity contest, but the person doesn't walk who wouldn't rather be held in high esteem than be hated, and that is why it takes a degree of valor to stand there naked and willingly expose yourself to a merciless berating. It is so easy to shove your conscience into a pocket and hand out ribbons; after all, it is only a class, who will notice? You, the judge, will notice, because you have told those people that this is a dog worthy of a badge of merit, and a blue ribbon is exactly that.

At the same show I encountered one of the saddest dog stories I've ever heard.

Late in the day, I was judging a group and my heart was turning between two excellent dogs. Unfortunately, there is only one blue ribbon, and a decision must be made. I made mine and gave second to a wonderful male whose owner told me, "This is this dog's seventh show. He has placed in the group seven times and he still doesn't have a point," there being no breed competition in that area. As my husband would say, "Wouldn't that frost your old potatoes?

Chapter 10

Tail Fanatics, Tooth Fairies and Negative Judging

The angry fist of winter is hammering at my door!

A mountain, to me, is an admirable backdrop and nothing to hurl myself from because it happens to catch the snow. There is no way that those wobbly ankles will support me, leaving ice skating, as far as I am concerned, to those who don't mind a cold, wet bottom. At heart, I am a palm tree and sailboat lady, yet inexplicably I return to the dubious appeal of New England.

Bowed beneath the prohibitive weight of oil price, we have acquiesced to the suggestion of energy conservators and installed a wood stove in our kitchen. This squat little presence is possessed of a rather cherubic, Victorian charm and the practicality enhanced by the fact that our house is set in wooded acres and our body-conscious, six-feet-two son actually enjoys chopping wood.

Dragging behind my writing machine and the requisite materials, I am nested beside my gurgling little friend to bring you what words I have. I am facing a window that looks me out on winter's picture and my private floor show. Bob has built a feeding station just below my eyes, and so the cardinals, juncoes, titmice and chickadees confer on the quality of our offerings in almost self-consciously Christmas-card posturing.

If you repeat this, I'll deny it: At this very minute, as my husband has kindly set a cup of tea at my side, the wood stove is murmuring and Henry, our adorable Teckel, is nestled at my feet, I concede to a measure of New England's harmony. We are just a few weeks from the Yule, Johnny Mathis is caroling "Sleigh Ride," and again Bob and I agree that this year we will test the lights before we string them, an annual promise that is never kept and each year we are faced with sullen little bulbs flaunting a dark visage as we set the stage for family gladness.

You may well ask, what has this to do with dogs? I sometimes wonder who reads my words or try to picture what they are doing when they turn their attention to me. Perhaps others wonder about such things, so it seemed appropriate to describe my position as I pen them.

Preamble has turned to amble, so to the subject at hand: priorities. Everyone who breeds, judges or handles believes in his right to preference, and so they may, but only if those priorities are based on educated conviction and not whim, or used as an exercise in evasion. And only then, if that conviction has a foundation of experience and in-depth study of the breed. This right to judgment must be earned.

Too often priorities are based on a single line in a standard. Too many good dogs have been flushed down the drain because some self-imposed celestial being has decreed him damned for a single infraction of the written ideal.

There is an untenable plethora of splendid dogs who are discarded because of a sub-standard detail, damned to perdition by shortsighted arbiters who admit to hang-ups. There are some who boast, "I will never put up an Afghan Hound who has no ring in his tail."

Everyone would love a backyard full of beautiful ringed tails, but isn't it of greater import to consider where the tail emerges from the body? I mean, in this day of cosmetological expertise, isn't it absurd to denounce a superior dog who lacks a loop at his nether end?

This is the kind of negative judging that urges people to the corner drug store and a roll of adhesive tape.

The most prevalent form of fault judging is manifest in the unrestrained capriciousness of some judges in regard to teeth. There are breeds whose very being depends on sporting forty-two perfectly aligned teeth; they don't concern me. I am bothered by the unbridled self-righteousness of those who apply those precepts to the Afghan.

Please don't misunderstand, full dentition in perfect alignment is a thing of beauty and much desired if all else is equal. My argument is with breeders who discard or judges who penalize a dog that surpasses others in every aspect except bite. Arbiters are quick to seize on an iffy bite or missing teeth as a reasonable explanation for their obliquity in judging. It's so easy, and who is to deny the rationale?

Damn it, the bite is just one part of a dog and only one, and must be weighed as such. Is the thought of missing teeth so repugnant that one with straight shoulders, short legs or a sagging topline is to be preferred, all in defiance of the standard? There are judges who boast that no dog with the tiniest flaw in his mouth will ever get a ribbon from them. These devastators of type do their work well, but do they know that among the savant they are dubbed "tooth fairies"?

We are deluged with people for whom the purple ribbon is a passport to immortality. His authority cannot be challenged, his conclusions are undisputable, there is no weighing process in this mind that victoriously falls upon a flaw and holds it up for the world to see. I wonder sometimes if a bite undetectable from ringside is not used as a happy excuse for poor judging. Does anyone ever question a judge who pontificates that he put a certain dog down for a faulty bite, not to question the presence of the dreaded bite but the importance of it vis-a-vis an untypical structure? OK, so one dog beat the other because he

Though Afghan Hounds were her first breed, Babbie also had an interest in the Dachshund, which was the breed she spent her later years with.

had a perfect mouth, but what good are forty-two teeth to a dog that can't catch the prey? Perhaps he uses that perfect ring tail to trip his quarry?

We have all succumbed to fault judging. So many years ago that I'm sure the owner doesn't remember, I put a lovely type dog down to a lesser one because he had a faulty mouth. I wish I could go back and do it over. I can't, but I did some soul searching. I researched my motives and found them lacking.

There is a current dog in the show scene who has, in modern nomenclature, four or five major reserves. It is the awareness that this beautiful animal is being subject nationwide to thoughtless adjudication that has prompted me to the written protest. Because of one component in an otherwise splendid dog, he is being defeated by some who are, in every other aspect, inferior. Because his bite is not perfect he is doomed. Wrong, I say, wrong!

It is said that the perfect dog is yet to be born, so let us consider what fault is the least of the evil. Let's take a long look at one who proudly bears his heritage with all parts functioning as they should to fulfill his purpose and ask ourselves: Is an Afghan nothing but a set of perfect teeth?

Spare me the woeful litany of genetic trap. Draw me no dread pictures of future generations of bulldog-mouthed Afghans. If such a danger were rampant, it would be far more prevalent than it is today. Without belaboring my memory or raising a hand to research, I can think of three wonderful, famous champions, all superb dogs, each in a far remove from the other, who exerted tremendous influence on the dogs of today. All three in disparate areas triumphed, flushing the prejudice of callous judging off in tides of respect. All three were used carefully and beneficially for the breed as we see it today. Almost all pedigrees of our present day include one, two or all three of these dogs. Yet each had a mouth of debatable perfection. I suppose some of the recent generations have inherited the weakness, but on the whole the influence of these dogs has been lifesaving to a breed that has verged on endangerment.

Fearing that erroneous conclusions will be evinced, accusatory fingers pointed and thoughtless debate incurred, I will not name this triumvirate. They were the progenitors of much of what is fine in the Afghan of today; they were and still are of irreplaceable value and have helped mold the best of today.

Our experience has to tell us that we are fools to listen to the purveyors of doom, who lead us down the path of mediocrity.

When experience is powerless, all things are the same.

Chapter 11

As the Days Dwindle Down for Sunny

A eulogy for Sunny, that's what was asked of me, and I guess that I am the logical one. Sunny and I go back a lot of years and have traveled a lot of roads together. They've not been without potholes, but I wouldn't have missed a minute of it.

My dictionary defines eulogy as, "A set oration of commendation as of the services of someone deceased."

Now, how do I wrap that around Sunny?

Do I say, Sunny was laughter? She was.

Do I say, Sunny was a tempest? She was.

Do I say, Sunny was wise? She was.

Do I say, Sunny was naïve? She was.

Do I say, Sunny was ruthless? She was.

Do I say, Sunny was generous? She was.

Do I say, Sunny was cunning? She was,

Do I say, Sunny was tough? She was.

Do I say, Sunny was gentle? She was.

Do I say, Sunny was music? She was.

Do I say, Sunny was discord? She was.

Do I say, Sunny was worldly? She was.

Do I say, Sunny was a child? She was.

Do I say, Sunny was a lady? She was.

Do I say, Sunny was gypsy? She was.

Sunny was light and dark and brilliance and obtuseness and obstinacy and credulity.

Sunny was – How can I say, Sunny *was*? Sunny *is*.

As long as there are Afghans bred, Sunny will be. Sunny's immortality is

Babbie Tongren awarding Best of Breed to Ch. Shirkhan of Grandeur, breeder-owner-handled as always by Sunny Shay at the 1960 Westminster Kennel Club Show.

where she would have it, in almost every Afghan that steps in a ring everywhere, and certainly in the top ones. How many are there that don't trace their ancestry to Grandeur someplace? How few there are who don't proudly boast of Shirkhan in what is otherwise sometimes a mundane pedigree. I have often laughed at the newcomer who in an attempt to impress, brags of Shirkhan, maybe he was six generations back, but even the rawest recruit to our ranks know this is a name to respect. Sunny and Shirkhan: a sometimes ragtag but always electric team who brought vitality to everything they touched.

Sunny and Shirkhan who on that miracle night in 1957 stood in the center of Madison Square Garden as the most respected judge of them all proclaimed them "Best in Show" at Westminster. When Bea Godsol, whose word no one ever questioned, refused to recognize the inalienable right of the prosperous elite who traditionally claimed top honors in that most illustrious of shows, she breathed new life into a jaded sport.

All the "little people" who saved all year to be there, who couldn't afford professional handlers or expensive equipment, who hadn't the money to buy top dogs so bred their own, all reached out to Sunny. She'd given them hope. "If Sunny can do it, so can I."

Oh, there was dissension and jealousy, no one more envious than I, but typically, Sunny had worn uncomfortable shoes that day, and as she often did, had borrowed mine. The knowledge that my shoes went Best in Show at Westminster has comforted me over the years. That is as close as I'll get.

Sunny Shay with judge Bob Tongren.

To grapple the essence of Sunny, and corset it into words is like asking Mercury to behave. To define her to someone who didn't know her is like telling a man about water who had never touched it. You could love her and you could hate her – no one ever ignored her. To paraphrase the song, "She may have been a headache but she never was a bore."

Sunny loved living. She has dragged me through amusement parks, and bullied me into sharing all of their dubious entertainments. I loathe amusement parks, but somehow with Sunny, even the loop de loop was fun. She has left me with torn and bleeding feet because nothing would do but shell hunting on the Pacific

Beach. I still have some of the shells. I have suffered poison ivy chasing after her through fields of wild blackberries.

Her curiosity was insatiable. I remember her driving one poor man to distraction until he had explained and demonstrated every facet of his work, blowing glass animals. She would pounce on anything that she didn't quite understand, no matter how seemingly irrelevant, and worry it, terrier like, until it was hers, stowing it away for some future use.

How Sunny loved food! The Abraham Lincoln Hotel, in Reading, Pennsylvania, must have teetered on bankruptcy after being host to us one evening. She heard of their justifiably famed buffet, and insisted we partake. Suffice it to say that after as many trips to the table as her conscience would allow, she bulldozed me into filling her plate three more times. She would bemoan her size, protesting that she really ate very little. Funny part was that she believed it.

Moderation played no part in Sunny's life, she burst from one day to another. There was no fear in tomorrow. No threat of world upheaval jittered her heart. The earth from pole to pole was hers to probe. She attacked everything with a zeal as to make a lesser mortal quail. She was as exultant about winning a puppy match as she had been about Westminster, and inconsolable did she lose.

So much a part of the dog show scene, she wore the cloak of host to many a frightened newcomer. In the days of benched shows, when someone new would betray their bewilderment and shyness, they often found their dog snatched from their hands and attached to the bench, and themselves engulfed in warm if boisterous welcome. I don't think Sunny ever refused help to anyone; often an untrained dog found himself expertly guided around a ring no matter his conformation qualifications.

This, then, was Sunny as I knew her. There is so much more that I have left unsaid. I wanted to tell of the plane ride we shared, and the strange, white-faced, black-haired beauty who sat behind us, almost immobile, and holding a nearly life-sized doll created in her image and dressed identically, and the uncanny part when we landed, there was no trace of either. We talked of that two weeks ago at dinner.

I wanted to tell of that lustrous early morning when Bob and I watched silently, as Sunny with my two sons, then little babies, each tucked under an arm, bobbed gently up and down in the pool, as she smiled tenderly down into their joyous faces. It was Mother Earth, and the beauty has come down twenty years with us.

We speak of it still.

We were there on that black Sunday in Connecticut. I had been with her minutes before she died, and when she fell into Sandy Schwartz's arms only the thought, "Sunny can't die, she'll be back next week," sustained me.

Friends and foes watched in horror and clung together. No one wanted to leave.

Boots Bellamy, always a superlative handler, took over her Ch. Boy Blu of Grandeur, and won the group with him. Dog and man worked together as if they knew that she'd never do it again. This was for Sunny.

People said things like, "The end of an era," "A legend in her time," "It's the way she would have wanted to go." I guess all of that is true – but not yet.

Chapter 12

Garden Club

Want to boggle your mind? Here's an exercise in 14-carat, stem-winding, mind-boggling thought. Imagine, if you can, an entire segment of the nation's population rolling about in gleeful anticipation of their annual trip to purgatory.

Dynamite!

If you doubt the purgatorial implication, try describing this safari to your pillar-of-society, church-going, dinner-on-the-table-at-six neighbor, who, if he believes you at all, will probably use a stronger term to define the destination.

Slice it as you will, the results are the same. Weeks ahead of post time, when the entry is mailed and the closing date passed, the gut torture digs in. Anxious hours of torment about the weather, of leaving loved ones well equipped with fuel oil, food, transportation, baby sitters, dog sitters, antifreeze and snow-removal facilities. The certainty that the wrong dog is entered as Dipthong is readied for the big time. More than likely Dipthong goes along with train of thought.

The fever is epidemic and national so I won't try to describe the problems of transportation, just to say that travel in winter is always Russian roulette, be it the Iron Bird, Amtrack's tortuous innovations, or the iffy family van. All of this with the added fillip of consoling the inconsolable, one, two or more confused and reluctant dogs.

There are dozens of specialties on the Westminster weekend, so most arrive in Sin City on Friday. This is where the masochistic yearnings begin to bear fruit. Trouble is immediate if you are driving. With fortune smiling you might just find a garage within eight blocks of the hotel at a cut-rate cost of $30 a day.

No New York taxi driver wants to know you with this incumbent cargo, and so it's eight blocks of hauling crates and dragging dogs who refuse to cooperate with New York curb laws. If you escape the $50 fine, chances are the interminable trek through filthy slush will terminate with the confrontation of a hostile room clerk, who, without looking up, smilingly assures you that, "There are no reservations in that name."

That tangle unsnarled and a room attained, to Dipthong's great relief. He couldn't wait to get in out of the cold to relieve himself as frantic owner tries to become a screen between him and the probing eyes of the bell boy.

A midtown hotel … now that is Nirvana – overcrowded, dirty and be prepared to leave five months of grocery money when checking out. I am sure better service is to be had at the Salvation Army. The one I have in mind is particularly popular with the dog set, and achieves an apex in inefficiency. We stayed there once, dismayed to find no towels. We had the effrontery to ask housekeeping for some and don't think we weren't treated like lepers for this impudence. Did you ever dry yourself on a sheet and then get in bed?

The elevators suffer from a delirious ennui and take turns working. It's hanging around or climbing eleven flights.

While regaling old George Stalwart, next door, with your fun time, don't forget the joys of getting something to eat. New York is replete with marvelous restaurants, which can be gotten to by cab at $7 a linear foot, if you can get one to stop. J. Paul Getty would feel the pinch after a week in New York restaurants.

I remember one year when the Afghan Specialty was on Saturday and a blizzard sneaked in on little cat feet, absolutely crippling the city and making any thought of leaving the hotel an impossible dream. Fortunately, my good friends Midge and Roy Horn assured me that they had a commodious room and would share it with me. It took but minutes for the word "commodious" to spread and we had lots of friends. Being a man of infinite ingenuity, Roy snooped a bit and found the housekeeper's cache: voilà, folding cots, sheets and towels! The roomiest hotel accommodations are hard pressed to accommodate 13 people and dogs, but this one did for days. We had a blast! The hotel kitchen, inadequate at best, ran out of food with the second snowflake. By acting quickly and boldly, we solved this by patrolling the corridors. You wouldn't believe the good stuff people leave on room-service trays.

Try that one on the Garden Club!

Monday … it's *Garden time.* Westminster had lost a lot of its charm with the passing of the old house over on Eighth Avenue. The new Garden is so clean and business like. See how dog-show people think? The new Garden seemed even newer this year. Visser and Visser had taken over and performed glories of newness and elegance. Brilliant green carpeted benches and wider aisles for all the annual reunions, the clusters of exhilarated winners and gathering of mourners. The crowing of triumphs, and the alibis for losses, reverberated through the brightness, too bright. I found it all depressing. I longed for the shabby, crowded old hall.

Monday, and Afghan time. Anne Rogers Clark, a splendidly impressive lady of resolute demeanor and firm convictions, presided. We shared a box with Judy

The height of Afghan Hound success at Westminster was Sunny Shay's Best in Show win in 1957 under Bea Godsol with Ch. Shirkan of Grandeur.

and Herman Fellton, Carol Duffy and Frank LaGreca. It is sometimes for the questionable good of those concerned, do Judy and I spend time together. We definitely bring out the worst in each other, and on occasions such as this, when a degree of dignity is in order, we tend to lapse into outrageous irreverence and gales of girlish giggles can be heard. I guess it's unbecoming for two matrons of our years and position, but we both enjoy it. I mentally saluted Mrs. Clark at the handling of her Winners Dog, a very nice young black-masked cream who had showed beautifully in his huge class. However, when Winners was circling the ring a handler behind the dog fell and obviously startled him. Afghan like, he dropped his tail and showed his dismay. Mrs. Clark, being aware of the situation, made no issue of it and quickly awarded him Winners. Many lesser judges would have jumped at the chance to negate the dog. It was in Glorvina Schwartz's Sandina Spellbound that she found her best Afghan.

Bob Tongren was asked to present the Roger Rechler/Dennis Sprung Sunny Shay

The Sunny Shay Memorial Trophy, a subject of some controversy in Afghan circles after her death.

Memorial Trophy to the winner, and was delighted to be rewarded by a kiss from Glorvina.

Okay, enough of all the sweetness-and-light society-page reporting – here comes the nitty, closely followed by some very gritty.

The trophy I have just mentioned is a beautifully executed statue of Shirkhan, who we all know went Best in Show, guided by Sunny, at the very show in 1957. The only Afghan, and one of only two hounds to ever shine at the top of the Garden's mightiest tree. When the decision was made to yearly commemorate the day that Afghan's wonder pair took that date and made it theirs, what more appropriate place than here. Westminster, rightly, has choice of special awards at their prestige show, but they did give permission for this one, with the proviso that permission be had from the Afghan Hound parent club before the trophy could be presented inside the ring.

Sounds easy? Not so ... For reasons understood only by that august governing body, permission was withheld. Last year when the award was initiated, I was asked to be the presenter and did so, *outside* of the ring. I felt ridiculous and a bit like an uninvited child pressing her nose against the window of a party when I had to swim upstream against the mass of exiting dogs and handlers to bestow upon the unprepared winner a rather heavy statue. The occasion lost its meaning and I my dignity.

Dennis and a few others have tried in vain to combat the prejudice of the worthy directors, emphasizing the enormity of the honor to the breed that Sunny and Shirkhan had brought with this unparalleled victory, and how fitting to perpetuate the glory with the presentation *in the ring*, at the show where it came to pass. Again permission was withheld. If there is logic in their motive, no one seems to have described it. The years have illustrated very little in the way of logic from the Afghan Hound Club of America. Ye gads, most breed clubs would leap for joy if one of their breed were to be so honored. The thing that interested me most was that Judy Fellton, who is delegate from that marvelous organization, was totally unaware of what had to have been a major decision, and she, too, seemed as appalled as I. There, I've gone and let them upset me again.

Back to the Garden Club … Having described how you and a sizeable section of society spend a week in February, there is no way that you are going to make them understand why. Fact is, I don't quite understand it. Never a year goes by, and I am coming up on 35, that I don't wildly proclaim to anyone interested, a few who could care less, "Not this year – no way. I can't afford it. I am sick, etc." As usual that week in February of this year found me doing business at the same old stand. I haven't shown a dog in years, which puts me in a questionable spot on the insanity scale of one to ten. Why would an otherwise reasonably bright woman put life, serenity and pocketbook on the line with absolutely nothing to gain?

Why? Because it's Westminster, that's why. Westminster is an irresistible ultimate. It is a breeder's dream and an exhibitor's nightmare. Only one among many shows, it takes but three judges to catapult a dog to BIS, as do the others. More often than not the judging is unfathomable, noted as killer of giants; most of the heads of top dogs fall along the way. I am glad to say that the past couple of years have proved the exception to what was once precedence. Last year I saw good dogs winning and reputations upheld. Each group was won by really good, well-handled dogs. It was refreshing.

Westminster is magic, folly, stardust. It is heartbreak and ecstasy, fun and pain. It's all the greats under one roof. Remember a few years back when the two top-winning Doberman sisters met head on? One from the east and the other from California. The crowd around that ring was deep. Again this year, the two Standard Poodle bitches, the much-talked-about Greyhounds and so on. Thrilling!

Westminster is theater, its judges all gussied up in evening clothes, TV cameras, spotlights. Its crowds hushed by the suspense, the vast arena a stage for incomparable drama, and the auditorium stilled. People speak in whispers and walk lightly, not even a dog barks until the final moment when the great decision is made. Then, throat-bursting cheers from the victor. Reality is the foot sore, bankrupt, bronchial let-down of the trip home. Anyway, that's Westminster. Now, explain that to the Thursday Bridge Club.

Chapter 13

Trophy Lives

If Paul Revere hadn't been so busy careening about town on his horse, disturbing the whole neighborhood, he might have had more time to stay home and tend to his silversmithery – and, just possibly, to come up with something besides the ubiquitous Revere bowl. I suppose it is reasonable to assume that at the time he fashioned it he didn't have dog-show exhibitors in mind, and I presume, in a normal society, there may be one or, at the most two, Revere bowls to a family – attractive, well polished and useful for fruit or flowers. However, lo the poor dog family who, after a few years of showing, finds themselves with wall-to-wall Revere bowls. At one time I counted, on shelves, in trunks, as food bowls, etc., 49 Revere bowls.

I've never had the heart to count trays. All I know is that if I were to entertain the whole cast of "Cleopatra," I'd still have more trays than hors d'oeuvres. They range in size from microscopic to three feet across. I had the only kids on the block with silver-plated flying saucers. They also make very elegant bird baths.

Recognizing a redundancy, and being tired of moving tarnished silver from the couch to chair in order to sit down, the mind dwells on finding good homes for some of it. This is not always as easy as it might seem. By the time the surplus has been recognized as such, and the urgency to deal with it has become apparent, we have also run out of non-doggy friends to whom we once might have palmed off a moderately undented piece of silver as a wedding gift. All there is left are companions of the show ring, all of whom know a trophy when they see one.

On the dubious proviso that you can find a trophy that is neither engraved or has taken such a beating on the way home from a show by rattling around in the back of a station wagon as to have lost its original shape and luster, it is possible to re-donate it to some grateful club for presentation at their show. This, of course, does have a twofold advantage: You unload a silver-plated incumbent and

Modern trophy table. The fetish for silver-plated bowls has, happily, finally abated.

simultaneously are made to feel like Santa Claus. This is not an original thought with me. I have had several old friends pass through my hands two or three times on their way to a final resting place.

A friend of mine, being more idealistic than I, reprimanded me for grumbling about useless trophies. She said I shouldn't want the dogs to furnish the house. Why not? They unfurnished it! I figure as long as they are up, they might as well win something handy.

A long time ago, the Providence Kennel Club gave electric percolators for first place in each group. I was of course elated to have it. It did look funny when we were all in for Best in Show and there were six owners standing around the ring with coffee pots poised in mid-air, for all the world like a soup kitchen.

I hope the preceding paragraphs have not sounded too ungracious. It is not without gratitude that I accept the winning that my dogs have done. As one who started an amazingly successful career as a breeder by showing a dog on a clothesline, and who asked the judge where he wanted me to put him when I

Trophy table at the Afghan Hound national specialty in Babbie's era.

was told to move my dog, I have not a complaint in the world. This is simply a tentative query as to why a trifle more imagination can't be displayed when it comes to trophies.

Having served a term or two as trophy chairman for various clubs, I know what a thankless job it is. I know how it feels to cut a swathe through a crowd at ringside, with everyone suddenly becoming very busy or looking in any direction but yours once the word gets around that it is collection time. It doesn't take long to make you feel like Oliver Twist's impoverished relative.

The tiresome burden of the trophy chairman's tasks more often than not is foisted off on a new and unsuspecting member of a club, who, being naïve enough to think it's better than wielding the pooper-scooper, and anxious to see his name in the premium list, eagerly agrees to take on this bummer of a job. The fallacy of this reasoning is that, while everybody is glad to see the guy with the pooper-scooper, nobody wants to know the one with his hand out. "I gave at the office" doesn't hold water at a dog show.

Desirous as he may be to do a bang-up job for his club, the chances are that our newly appointed chairman of the goodies is involved in a single breed with an acquaintanceship extending to other breeders within that breed or at the most within the group to which that breed belongs. Hence, he finds himself tapping on the shoulders of those with whom he is familiar, and the other five groups go ignored. So it is that, be the trophy chairman an exhibitor of Dobermans, the premium list is apt to sport three pages of trophies for Dobermans and the rest come under the heading of "Five dollars for all classes including twenty-three or more."

Loathe to criticize without a form of construction, I hereby offer a solution to the imbalance of awards at most shows. This is not original with me. I have seen more than one club function in this manner, but it was at Waukesha that I saw it with my own eyes. I haven't an idea of what manner of coercion Al and Esme Treen use. Somehow they run a club with as many members working as there are members. Whether it is the rack, thumb screws or simple charm, they pull it off and, as anyone knows who heads a club, this is a neat trick. Their solution to the trophy problem is not one, but six trophy chairmen, or one for each group. I can't say for sure, but I imagine that each of these is involved in that group for which they are working and so, familiar with the exhibitors and breeders within the periphery of their own interest. It is a lot harder to say "no" to someone you stand next to every week than it is to a total stranger. The result is a premium list that is only a few pages thinner than the Los Angeles telephone book.

There is a measure of Uriah Heap in all of us, and carting home a bit of material evidence of victory to impress the neighbors can often tip the scale of whether to enter or not. There are many other factors in the outcome of a successful show, but certainly this is one to be considered, especially when attempting to attract the novice or single-dog exhibitor and, let's face it, these are the people who comprise the backbone of any show. These are the ones who swell the entry.

Now that I have pummeled quantity into the ground, let's get back to quality. With due respect to the generosity of those who offer silver or silverplate, may I suggest a soupcon of imagination would be appreciated. There were times in my showing career that I was convinced that dog shows were subsidized by Messers Gorham. Personally, my most treasured relics are objet d'art and some not so d'art, but that represent something to which I can relate. Something that is reminiscent of the breed that I am showing or the occasion of triumph. Besides the vast accumulation of silver and plate, I have been fortunate to acquire an enviable collection of ceramics ranging in quality from the expertise of Kay Finch to some barely recognizable amateur efforts.

After these many years of kids, and dogs, most have been glued together so often that close inspection is not tolerated. They still represent more to me than all the sterling that Tiffany can produce. In the old "anything goes" days, there have been some pretty bizarre trophies. The one that comes to mind was offered many years ago, when the Best of Breed trophy in Old English Sheepdogs was a live sheep.

Do I have to add that it was won by some hapless souls who resided in a New York City apartment? It was just about then that the AKC took a hand and restricted the originality of donations.

There is no way that I can talk about delightful and imaginative trophies without mentioning the Afghan Hound Club of Houston specialty, which Kay Finch and I judged a few years back. Never have I seen nor hope to see a comparable display. A little money, and a great deal of love and talent, went into creating the cleverest assortment of figurines imaginable. Conceived and executed by Johanna Tanner, a dedicated member of the club, they were spectacular. Employing a technique that I believe is her own, she evidently builds the little figures by using a soldering gun of some sort, dripping the metal into a shape and applying a gold finish. Each of the first prizes was meaningful to its appropriate class. The brood bitch was mommy with some young, and if you want to know what the stud dog was, check with Peter Belmont. It brought the house down. All were mounted on a stunning stone base. No less awe inspiring were some lovely hand-painted ceramics by Derrellyn Adams Yates. Both Kay and I were lucky enough to receive some of each of these, along with a needlepoint head study by Dale Lavaque. This took your breath. Richard Souza from California went Best of Breed and last seen, he was lurching about with a glazed look pondering how to get his vast assortment of glories, which included an enormous soup tureen, safely back along with himself and dogs. I must find out how he managed.

A final comment on the subject, and at the risk of being thought overly sophisticated or under financed, a small envelope containing cash is always pleasant and hardly ever gets dented en route home.

Chapter 14

Happy Wanderers

OK, OK, Jonathan Swift, pull up an ear and sit down. It's time that you were clued in on a few expeditions that make your narrative pale. You thought old Gulliver's travels were so much that he took some hazardous trips, made some wild turns, and ran into some freaky people. Well, compared to some dog-show judges, his feet were dragging.

To contemplate the misadventures of our all-rounders, who weekly brace themselves for chaos and accept overwhelming odds against an uneventful trip while plying their trade, is to make one faint with disbelief.

I don't claim kinship with these courageous souls whose idea of a triumphant weekend is to arrive on the same plane with his luggage.

An eye to my phone bill keeps me from personally contacting more of our in-demand adjucators, but I am sure that Henry Stoecker alone could fill an encyclopedia. Here are a few of the Tongren sagas, as well as some I've picked up along the way.

Dedication is in large part the key to "What makes Sammy run." It is also the answer to skeptics who ask, "Why must the show go on?" Well, of course, a nice fat check from the show chairman helps grease the wheels.

About as dedicated as you can get was our good friend Howard Tyler, who several years ago accepted an assignment to judge Westminster, since that worthy institution is notoriously reluctant to lay out a farthing. Now I am sure everyone will remember that year when some irreverent demon took hold of the usually compliant God of the Garden and Specialties weekend, and teased him into hurling all the foul weather at hand upon us, and then went out and borrowed some more. The blizzard was a doozey! Those who were in New York stayed there and those who weren't cried. I recall meeting Joe Tacker, who at the time lived in Hawaii, and had flown in for the Garden. Others would call it madness, we call it dedication.

Back to Howard, who lived in Connecticut, just a spit away from Gotham, and so had waited for the morning of the show to jog on over. The jogging proved impossible. Everything was stilled by four feet of nasty, stick-in-throat, "I'm not going to move and neither are you" snow!

Cars, planes, buses and dog sleds met their Waterloo. Mrs. Tyler told me some time later that, exhausting every possibility, Howard had evidently said, "Uncle," or so she thought, when she became aware of a thumping from the attic. What else? Howard was digging out some of the kids' discarded snowshoes. He was going to walk to New York. He didn't, but it's a beautiful picture.

The problems besetting our happy wanderers are varied and many. To dredge out a few at random … recognition.

Somewhere about 50,000 feet in the air comes the chilling realization that the warm and welcoming voice on the phone who had volunteered to meet you has no face, and there is no reason to assume that they know yours. Most veteran club members shift the meeting detail off on the eager novitiates. Were they to come to the gate, or be at the desk? Security has cut this down, but I have spent breathless hours sprinting through airports, trying to unscramble the P.A.'s garblings. Are they blaring, "Paging Mrs. Tongren" or "Flight 202 now boarding"? It took a lot of near misses, but I finally hit upon a solution. Now I carry a premium list of the show in front of me. Once a smart club member who had anticipated the problem met me holding an Afghan pup.

One night of horror was spent in a small but spiteful airport in the South. Donning my best "Aren't you lucky to have me" smile, I tripped off the plane and into an empty building … unoccupied desks, no passengers, luggage masters or ticket takers. It was a real Rod Serling trip. Eventually a janitor and his broom came into sight, but he was either from the Deep South or didn't speak any English at all. No way to tell. Of course I hadn't brought the club's correspondence with me, and had not the faintest idea where my motel was. When I tried to call the one person in town I knew, I found my resources to be a $20 bill. Did you ever hate a $20 bill? Well, try pushing one in the slot that says "one dime." An angel in the guise of a long-haired teenager materialized. I guess the poor lad was scared half out of his wits when he found himself encircled by a jabbering madwoman babbling, "I'll give you a $20 bill in exchange for a dime." Recovering his poise –

Ch. ben ghaZi Mariyah The Black with Louise Levine. *Photo courtesy Sighthound Review/Bo Bengtson*

the boy had class – he smiled, handed me a dime and vanished into the night. My sons never did understand my about-face on long hair.

Irrelevantly, I am reminded of the time my sister spent an incautious evening out with the girls. Bugged by an uneasy conscience, she called her husband. Her first defeat came when the telephone obdurately refused to swallow the olive from her martini, which she was trying to feed in in lieu of the dime that she didn't have. Once the call was transacted the dialogue went like this: Jerry (husband): Where are you? Pat (sister): Can you hear the jukebox? Jerry: No. Pat: Then I'm in the library.

O'Hare Airport alone could provide meat for a weighty volume. Personally, I will gladly detour through Mexico City to avoid that massive confusion. So delicately planned is O'Hare that there is no circumstance under which a three-mile hike is avoidable when changing planes.

A deep-rooted conviction that airline personnel are crusading to provide clothes for the needy has convinced me that if I ever want to see my clothes again I'd best carry on my own bag. I figure that if it won't fit in my small, seedy suitcase, I don't need it. So if my right arm appears to be six inches longer than the left, it's because of the many miles of charging through O'Hare Airpot, toting the wretched bag.

There was a New Englander friend who was slated to judge someplace in Texas. It seems his travel agent had booked him on a flight that terminated in Georgia, and it was only after endless hours of hanging around that he finally consummated his journey at 2 a.m., in some out-of-the-way place in Texas. There was no way that he could rouse anyone who even wanted to know him, never mind help him get transportation to the city of his destination, which was some twenty miles up yonder. To make this short, he finally came upon a lonely stranger who offered to sell him his horse for an outrageous figure. My friend swears the horse was on his way to the glue factory. Anyway, picture if you can, this dignified gentleman from New England's upper strata, arriving at the show many hours later covered with dust astride a Don Quixote reject.

Obviously a one-shot deal, I did beat the airlines at their own game once. I was to meet my husband, who was coming in on another flight, at the gate of our connecting one. Experience had taught me that if I wanted to avoid a brisk four-mile hike I had better think fast. My theater training had taught me in good stead, and I visibly weakened in view of the stewardess. I wish you could have seen Bob's face when his hitherto healthy wife came into sight, propelled at great speed in a wheelchair. I wonder if they would remember me.

If anyone questions the existence of a genie created to deter the footsteps of dog-show judges on their appointed rounds, let them figure this one. As I usually do when judging in California, I planned to go a few days ahead and spend some time with my family, who live in Fallbrook. Though a charming town, Fallbrook really isn't on the way to anywhere and you can't get there from here. The trick is to land in Los Angeles or San Diego and rent a car for the trip north or south, as the case may be. An opportunity to spend an extra day arose, and I changed the reservations for the car and plane the night before I left. Once in L.A., I presented my eager little face at the desk of those who were frantically trying harder, only to be told that, "Mrs. Tongren picked her car up an hour ago." No one but the airline, Avis and I knew of my schedule change. You'd better believe that that rotten genie was driving that weekend instead of bombing around in a bottle.

Anything involving Sunny Shay was colorful. No exception was one of the many trips that we shared some years ago. There seemed to be an inordinately long wait for departure after the doors had closed. Finally, the pilot announced that due to mechanical difficulties, take-off would be delayed a smidgen. Two hours went by while we waited for what we thought was a new engine to be flown in. Finally the doors opened to admit a rather small, grubby man carrying a Phillips screwdriver who bustled into the cockpit. Ten minutes later the engines revved, and we took off. Friends who had waited told us that after many calls from the pilot, our savior had been located in Harry's Bar & Grill. Never underestimate the power of a Phillips screwdriver.

Snow plays a major part in our careers, like the year it took us two cars and three hours to get to Hartford's First Governor Foot Guard Show … nine miles door to door.

If the airlines don't get you one way, they will another. Try the champagne flight to Florida. Mine left at 9:15 a.m. At 9:17 the steward is chirruping at your elbow, "Ready for champagne?" Now, I am rarely accused of being a stick in the mud, but to me that is a mite early for the bubbly. Some others felt as I did, and added their voices to mine in a touching plea for a simple cup of coffee to which the steward finally reluctantly complied, making no effort to hide his dismay. I want to tell you, that was a riotous group that disembarked in Miami into the alarmed arms of waiting friends.

Anyway, it's fun, awful, tiresome, exhilarating, boring and always different.

Chapter 15

Putting Your Money Where Your Mouth Is

I can't believe that I am doing this. I would have taken an oath that there was no power on earth that could move me to further protest. I truly believed that. I had spent such energy on this topic that my imperturbability was intact and nothing could intrude on my complacency. That's how much I knew!

The cries of "beating a dead horse" are even now pounding in my ears, but let me tell you something. If that horse is really dead, then fie on those who have killed it. I am just enough of an optimist that I may be kidding myself, but I think I can feel a faint pulse, and I will keep right on flogging until there is nothing left to flog with.

The response to my past articles on the subject of trimming was both gratifying and, in some cases, shocking. My response to the negative was, "What the hell, if that is what they want, forget the Afghan Hound as the lithe, majestic creature of the desert. Let them have that manufactured art-nouveau being that I see misrepresenting itself in the name of the 'King of Dogs.'" When I read the derisive letters, I made a point of watching the dogs shown by the authors. Of course that accounted for it: In each case the sculpted treasures were presented with no pretense of doing other than breaking all the rules: trimmed faces, backs, hocks and that ubiquitous rigidly straight underline that bears no resemblance to Mother Nature's intent. Why not? – they win!

Whatever happened to integrity?

My newly rekindled fervor is due to a recent show that we judged. I did Afghans on Saturday and Bob did them on Sunday. Churning along, dispensing as best I could with my other breeds, I got to Afghans. I saw a few familiar faces, but on the whole and with some relish I prepared myself for what I hoped would be an enlightening experience. Dogs went off fine, and I began to enjoy myself, having

Babbie breeder-owner-handling Ch. Karli ben ghaZi to the top at the Afghan Hound Club of America national specialty in 1955. From left, trophy presenter and Hollywood actor Charles Ruggles, club president Charlotte Coffey and judge Eugene Beck.

found a nice, reachy, young, long-necked, electric kind of dog for Winners; my kind of dog.

Just about then, the whole thing fell apart. Into my ring paraded a class of four puppy bitches. I couldn't believe what I was looking at … I am talking trimmed! Four poor little infants sporting the most artificial patterns that I have ever seen. All I could think of was that they resembled nothing more than four little girls dressed up in their mothers' high heels, sweet baby faces peeking through their hair – dogs with their lipstick smudged.

I am afraid that I was guilty of the most immature and unprofessional reaction. Suddenly and unexpectedly I was a long-time breeder and lover of Afghans. My cool went out the window and I lost my temper. Swept by rage at the arrogance of those people who were performing these obscenities on my breed, my seasoned objectivity deserted me as I ordered them all from the ring, withholding all ribbons. "All awards withheld," I marked my book. "Trimmed in defiance of the standard."

This may be called putting my money where my mouth is.

It so happened that there were several respected Afghan judges there that day who came to my ring, congratulating me and being supportive of my stand. I responded that if they truly approved, then it is their part to follow through. I had opened the door and if their convictions are as resolute as they claimed that day, they have but to step through it. I will be anxious to see how many will actually support their own declamations of artifice when faced with the actuality.

Before trying to blow me away again with irate responses, please, dear readers, picture to yourselves wherein lies my protest. It is not the adults whose natural pattern may have been cleaned up with strategic fingers, it is baby puppies who should be fuzzy and as yet unstructured. There is nothing cuter than a fluffy puppy and his whiskery face and soft cloudlike coat, and nothing of more pathos than those sad little bitches with the obvious clipper marks that carved a perfect three-inch saddle down the back and across the face.

It didn't take long for the word of my latest radical action to get back. Just last Sunday at Westchester I heard, "It was wonderful that you did it, but I'd never have the guts to risk popularity." *So* – this is a popularity contest? If so, it is one that I will never win and never want to. By worrying about exhibitor approval, judges are giving in and delivering their approbation of a deliberately executed insult to the judge himself and to a wonderful dog of antiquity, yes, and grace.

Now that I have covered ideology, let's talk feasibility. I have hit on this topic ad nauseum. I think I even promised the editors to lay off, but you have to admit that the point I am about to make is innovative and logical.

Without being berated for egotism, may I say I thought that almost every Afghan exhibitor by now would know my feelings on this subject and, if necessary, have the sense to avoid my ring like a case of typhoid. If they don't, they should –

for this reason. Anyone desiring to breed and/or show dogs of any breed should investigate every avenue of that breed. They should poke around among bloodlines before initiating their program and, once having settled on their desired type, they should uncover all there is to know about furthering their own goals.

In short, it only makes sense to glean every scrap of knowledge available before launching into a project as time consuming and expensive as breeding and showing dogs. The most readily accessible means of education is the written word. There is but a handful of books on Afghans and all are pretty old, so it seems apparent that before taking another step potential breeder-showers would subscribe to, and read, and study, the magazines on the topic of their hearts' desires.

This is why I suggest that anyone who has done their homework should be aware of my mores. I have written for *The Afghan Hound Review* for years and have denounced trimming lustily. So, even if they hate me (and I concede the possibility), the exhibitors should have made themselves conscious of how I in turn hate little baby puppies with tortured little hairstyles. Even if they disagree, they should use better judgment than to display their ineptitude for my opinion, and should they be so foolhardy, don't cry if they get zapped.

I am sure that a collector of fine porcelain bones up on the subject before dropping into an antique shop for a real find. It is inconceivable to me that with splendid publications such as this one available to them, the novitiate would not study the pictures and the articles before plunging into the icy waters of the dog shows.

My husband is, as everyone knows, more tactful than I. When confronted the following day with this class of toddlers, he was kinder. He remonstrated with the owners for being impatient and assured them that in time nature would take care of what they were forcing so awkwardly. He did dispense ribbons. Well, although Bob and I have a great life, one thing we have rarely agreed on is judging, and good sense has made us cautious of discussing our decisions. We each concede to the other the right of differing opinions, so I guess we aren't going to start agreeing now. Although I admire his gentle handling of a difficult area, there is no way that I would ever do differently than I did. I was warned that I was jeopardizing my future entries. Hey, guys, that's fine. I'd rather have five correct Afghans Hounds in my ring than seventy-five caricatures.

Before I don my battered golden helmet, pick up my crooked staff and ride off astride my aging nag, let me once more beseech these perpetrators who run afoul of Mother Nature: "Stop before there is no trace left of Rudiki, Rajah, Turkuman Nissim's Laurel, Karli, Shirkhan, Abraxas, Dragon Lady, etc., to remind us where it all began."

"Who are they?" you ask.

I rest my case.

Chapter 16

The End of the Story

To Jane Walker, who took the time to write, and to the many who verbalized their approbation, I send my thanks for the support they have given to what at best is a controversial stand, at worst an unpopular one.

To the disclaimers I will make just one more reply, and then I say, "Enough already." Frankly, I am bored to death with the people who have so little to do with their time, energy and stamps as to shell me with repetitious missiles. If the "professional steward" had bothered to check his facts, he might have been more aware of the mores of AKC, who is very firm about judges engaging exhibitors in lengthy discussion during judging. I did explain this in a previous article; however, my dissenters are so wrapped up in their breathy condemnations that they have not bothered to read. So, once again …

I did not disqualify the most disputed class. I wrote in my judge's book, "Dismissed for trimming in defiance of the standard." Get it? They were dismissed, not disqualified. I hope this is the last time that I have to go through all of this tedious explanation. *And* if trimming is not in defiance of the standard, what is? I would have been delighted to enlarge upon my position had any of these exhibitors remained until the complete program of judging was accomplished, I had other breeds to judge and did not want the AKC on my back for discussion of things not relevant to my schedule. Further, I was present the following day. Why didn't these people approach me then?

The "professional steward" claims to offer "an impartial view," however in the next paragraph he says he "did not show that day due to the reputation preceding" me… That's an impartial view?

People who fire off these missiles of condemnation really should check their facts. Again, I am accused of proclaiming a class of dogs as having been "razored."

These people are damned by their own hand, as they obviously have not read any of the preceding letters and articles carefully enough to rebut them. Once again, and watch my lips, I never mentioned the word razor, I have never heard the word applied to trimming an Afghan, didn't in fact know that this was done. So, "professional steward," in as much as you claim these words as a direct quote, I, ostensibly, according to your letter, said: "Those dogs have been razored, tell them they are excused." You have blown your own credibility and since this so-called direct quote was manifestly untrue, what reason would anyone have to listen to the rest of your poppycock? Oh, also, I did not write a word about lack of merit; remember, it was someone else who did.

A more thoughtful letter, but again one not researched, claims that I am discarding good dogs because of one superficiality such as trimming, which she considers an infraction of the rules. You are right, dear lady, it is just that however I have iterated and reiterated to the point of ennui, that my objection to trimming is not trimming itself but the reason for it. People (I avoid the term breeders) are breeding for coat with disregard for the essential, basic structure of the dog. They will argue that in order to win under the judges at an all-breed show your Afghan must be heavily coated, as the judge penalizes the sparsely coated dogs. I have always said that it is up to the breeders to educate the judges. If that is all they see that is what they honor. This leads to the penalty for dogs who are patterned, and what a shame this is. We can all thank God that this has not always been fact. Ch. Blue Boy of Grandeur was a very patterned dog, who today would have been tossed on the discard heap. Examine your pedigrees, most of you, and ask where you would be today … Blue Boy was Shirkhan's sire.

My priorities are not based on a single line but on a very real concern, which is defined in that single line – actually, two. If dogs were bred for the unique quality that is Afghan and not for hirsute redundancy, they would embody the desirable characteristics, such as croup (also extinct), layback, neck, and all of the linear definition that comprises the dog of antiquity. If these unique qualities were awarded topmost importance in breeding programs, then trimming would not be utilized to produce a dog that can win, but rather the winning could be done by a dog of proper properties.

I emphasize the adjective "unique"; so much is just that in our breed. It is "unique" to the Afghan to be clothed in two entirely separate coat textures. The saddle and coat on the face are harsh and short, and although we seldom see a break in the leg pattern anymore, that too is harsh and short. Remember the time when the neck had short hair on the sides that was not simply shaved to give the effect? I have heard people say that when the saddle has been trimmed there is no true saddle coat, simply a shaved back.

I believe if the beauticians continue their improprieties, in time there will be no two separate coats. As in the course of evolution fish discarded their legs, our breed will discard his coat pattern that sets him apart from others. My research has come up with only the Irish and American Water spaniels who share this trait. The face, neck, saddle and pastern patterns should be bred for, not against, and the mode so popular today of producing tons of hair with disregard for the original purpose will in time be unknown and the sculptor will emerge victor. It would be possible to take a Bearded Collie and carve a pattern and, voilà, there would be little difference.

Perhaps my priorities can be misinterpreted, perhaps through my own inability to define them. If indeed they are based on a single line, then I draw an analogy. The constitution of the United States is based on a single line. "Life, liberty and the pursuit of happiness" harnesses the entire concept of that all-important document; the rest is clarification on that concept.

By dismissing dogs that are trimmed I am trying to say, "Hey, you wouldn't take a Rembrandt and retouch it because the colors didn't suit your fancy." An Afghan is a work of art as described in the standard, which allows for patterning and describes a natural saddle and smooth face, so why must nature be improved on? It is not just one segment of the standard that I am upholding;

Ch. Blue Boy of Grandeur, above, sire of the great Shirkhan, below.

The Afghan Hound Review
MARCH APRIL 1975   THE STUD ISSUE

Ch. Shirkhan Of Grandeur
THE ALL TIME TOP SIRE

that segment, if noted, disallows breeding for coat alone because if that segment is followed, the importance will be where it belongs. If the coat breeders can't take the clippers and scissors to carve their own dogs, then and only then will their emphasis be placed where it belongs, on the basic conformation – because that is what is going to show. That is why it is up to breeder-judges to take a stand. By dismissing dogs they are in essence saying, "Now go home and breed one that conforms to the standard and quite trying to make your own."

My confirmation has been delightfully reinforced. Within the last four months I have judged Afghans four times, which is unusual as I have become reluctant to do so for the very reason that is emphasized here. I know my convictions are unpopular in some estimations, so it has been more politic to avoid judging the breed and the inevitable confrontation is sidestepped. I digress, back to my recent assignments. On all four occasions my Afghan entry has been the largest in the show, which proved to me that it can be done. Except for a minor exception I saw no trimming. I have not faulted dogs when it has been apparent that at one time their faces have been clipped and it was then growing in. Bravo, I say to these people. Possible the following day the clippers have been brought back into play, but for that moment they were as they were meant to be.

One more comment on that fateful day when I dismissed those puppies. To those who ask why I didn't do this in the earlier classes, I must ruefully admit that they are absolutely correct in questioning this. I guess I did a slow burn and it was not until those four bitches came into my ring that my resolution to act upon my angry refutation of this blasphemy was firmed. I should have started earlier, but somehow nothing in the earlier classes appeared so blatant. I have since and will in the future continue to follow my heart in active search for the real thing and to discard the manmade products.

I am happy to report that several people who judge Afghans have told me that they have already penalized trimming and will continue to do so. So like it or not, the natural state is returning, albeit slowly, but it is coming.

Now – I hope that some saner heads are as tired of all of this as I am, and just maybe they will consider that I have nothing in my being but love for the breed. I am not trying to be a martyr, I am certainly not self-aggrandizing. I am simply trying to turn around a very dangerous trend, and why can't you accept this as fact and concede that just possibly I may be making a valid and important point?

Chapter 17

Remembering The Silver Shadow

To a writer there is nothing more infuriating than an empty sheet of paper, and I have never faced one with more reluctance than now.

When I learned that a group of Blue's admirers were gathering funds to publish a memorial to him, I resisted, feeling that a precedent was being set and that anyone with a beloved pet who dies will want the same attention. Bless their hearts, his faithful fans used such terms as "special" and "influence on the breed" and like wonders, so I have relented and shall try to tell of him – so here is Blue.

To pretend that The Silver Shadow was the result of long-time planning would be untrue – he happened. Anyone who knows me well is aware that his mother, Apryl, was to me that special dog that most breeders have once, if they are lucky. She was my heart, and when she died I vowed that that was all for me as a breeder. Never again would I allow anything to hurt that much – nothing preventable, that is. So, let's start with how Apryl came to be.

In 1962, my daughter tragically had a baby who died, and she of course was inconsolable. At that time, Reigh Abram had sent Ch. Dureigh's Swan Song to me to show, and while he was here ben ghaZi's Bahia came in season. Only to help fill an aching void and assuage Pat's grief somewhat, we bred the two, and Pat took Bahia to care for. This was not irresponsible breeding. Swan Song was sired by Ch. Ben ghaZi's Mandingo and Bahia was his sister, both sired by Karli, so happily it made a degree of sense. I will never forget the morning that Pat called me and said, "Are you sitting down? If you're not, you'd better: Bahia just had seven white bitches."

After assuring me that she really could tell the difference and hanging up, I stared into bleak space wringing my hands in despair. Today this would not have been so catastrophic, but at that time self-masked creams or whites were held in contempt. I wound up giving away all but one, happy to find homes for them. The one was, of course, Apryl. It was with some defiance that we decided to show her and incredulously found that others shared our enthusiasm for her beauty and she finished handily.

At that time Ch. Khalife of Grandeur was around and my admiration for him was no secret, so giving in to the cry "You owe it to the breed to breed Apryl," I was persuaded, against my judgment, to unite the two.

ben ghaZi's The Silver Shadow, known to his friends as "Blue."

John and Judy Collette, who owned Khalife, whelped the litter, and on the day of the birth called, incoherent about the incomparable beauty of these pups. I attributed their passionate excitement to the overzealous first breeder until the day I went to gather up Apryl. There was no doubt; they were nine of the finest puppies I had ever seen. To cut an interminable story to wieldable size, tragedy again intervened and the litter was vaccinated with a faulty serum. Over an agonizing period of three months they faded away, leaving four. One exquisite bitch whose frontal musculation was afflicted, two incredibly healthy bitches, and Blue, whose blue eye ultimately developed into glaucoma and had to be removed.

Through other people who heard of our plight, we learned of several litters that had been vaccinated by the same vet and had met the identical fate; all but one of breeds other than Afghans. We put together this blood-curdling story: It seems

that the laboratory had dismissed two men who felt that their dismissal had been done in a cavalier fashion and to revenge themselves had deliberately sabotaged an entire vat of vaccine. Along with several others, we sued, and in court the two culprits admitted their dastardly work. We won the suit, but were left with the most exciting dog that ben ghaZi had ever bred but who could never be shown. To our astonishment, by word of mouth from people who had seen him at home, an interest in Blue as a stud began to shape. The rest is legend. I am not so naïve as to not realize that some of his popularity lay in the fact that not ever having been shown, he'd never beaten anyone and therefore nobody hated him. Happily, he did fulfill his promise and I believe

Ch. ben ghaZi's Apryl, dam of The Silver Shadow, facing page.

has been a beneficial influence on the Afghan of today.

Corsetting Blue into descriptive phrases is like trying to fit the wind into words for one who has never felt it. He believed that the world was created for his amusement. Dismayed by nothing, his life was for living.

Everyone who saw him employed the same adjectives: "Dynamic – electric – exciting – he moved as if on eggs – his feet spurned the earth." His head was always held high and his tail never down. Even after the trauma of two cornea transplants done by a famous human eye specialist at the Columbia Presbyterian Hospital in New York, his personality was unscathed. When his eye rejected the donor corneas, the good doctor wanted to try a third time, but we felt that Blue had been through enough and ordered the eye removed.

David Frost called one day, asking us to bring an Afghan into New York to appear on his TV show, and of course we selected our extrovert Blue. We arrived in town the night of the performance, and as I alighted from the car on 45th Street at about 8 p.m., right at the crowded theater hour, it struck me: "What have I done? This poor country bumpkin is going to be terrified." I looked down to

ben ghaZi's The Silver Shadow (second from left, with Babbie) winning the stud-dog class at the Colonial Afghan Hound Club show in 1972 under Sue Kauffman.

reassure my poor frightened friend and found myself holding an empty lead. Blue was standing on the curb having a conversation with a policeman's horse and greeting passersby in a manner befitting a mayoral candidate.

Because there was so much interest in him nationwide, we decided to enter him in the stud dog class at the Colonial Specialty at which Sue Kauffman was judging. When I entered the huge crowded building, again I was struck with terrible misgivings. The poor guy had rarely been out of the backyard and was scarcely lead broken, certainly he had no idea of what a show pose might be. I was sure that this time I had completely undone his libido and that he would be scared to death. Not to worry: I felt a tug on my skirt, and there he was, laughing and stamping his feet. "Oh, boy, Mom," he said. "Look at all the girls!"

Not one for small print, I hadn't noticed that the premium list made provision for but two get, and there we were with four grown, fully coated champions strung out behind. When the steward tried to stop me, I said, "To hell with this – come on, gang, let's go." After awarding us first, Sue said, "Get rid of the others and take him around alone. Let them see what a real Afghan looks like."

Needless to say, the ham in both of us responded. I dropped the lead, and Blue sailed around that ring like a veteran. The crowd got to their feet and cheered him. Everybody cried. Lawdy me, it was fun. I am sure that I don't have to tell you that there was a protest registered. I handed the ribbon and the trophy to the lady who had gotten second place and had made the protest. We had had our jollies.

Winnie Heckman, a splendid dog woman, a true lady, and a fine judge was visiting us for the first time when she looked out the window and saw Blue amid a score of others. For an instant I feared for her. I thought she was having a seizure. Seconds later she was out in the run, wading through strange dogs and running her hands over Blue. When she came in, she announced, "That is the greatest Afghan I have ever seen! He must be shown!" When we pointed out the technicality of his having but one eye, she answered, "There is nothing in the standard that specifies two eyes. If you ever see me doing the breed, the Group and BIS, you bring him. I have never said that before."

Of course Fate, who enjoys whimsies, took a hand, and shortly thereafter a premium list for Great Barrington, a show quite close to home, arrived with just such a slate as she had described. Oh, we were tempted, but, fearful for Winnie's reputation, we desisted. Wouldn't that have been fun, though?

So – there is Blue to those who knew and loved him. There is no way that I can speak of Blue without talking of Dianne and Red Roskosky, who took him to live with them and their beloved Banachek after the fire in our home. Many people have said, "When I die I want to come back as a dog belonging to the Roskoskys." To them we owe an unpayable debt of gratitude for the loving care that they lavished on The Silver Shadow.

Chapter 18

The Roar of the Greasepaint, the Smell of the Crowd

"How did you happen to get into dogs?"

This, more than any other question, is asked of we who are considered Old Timers in the sport. I tend to slough it off with a degree of shuffling and head scratching. Being a family thing it is hard to explain, unless you knew my family.

Though my own career in this foolishness has been primarily connected with Hounds, it was Sporting dogs that began the whole thing.

Centuries ago, when I was a child, my father, who was quite a successful actor, decided to play the part of the country squire and moved us from our suite at the Algonquin Hotel, which had been our permanent seat of operation. To that date his sole concession to the rural life was a summer cottage on Nantucket.

To one of his profession, proximity to New York was a must, and so it was that we settled in the wilds of Long Island. The idea of Long Island as a wilderness is probably inconceivable to the long-suffering commuters and beach freaks that turn today's highways into giant parking lots all summer.

We nestled in a charming sleepy little cul de sac entirely inhabited by theater people and their families. Our social life revolved about a private beach complete with supervision and best of all "The Community House" that was unique in that instead of traditional activities of such a meeting hall, i.e. dances, plays were staged by the professionals. Although the presentations were executed for and by the young people, incompetence and amateurism were not tolerated.

It must be brought to someone's consciousness that as good parents they should endow their children with a love for all things living, and somehow a dog show seems a likely start. Although dogs were prominent members of the community, few had been acquired with show potential in mind. Thus began the wildest run on purebred animals since Noah got it all together.

Kennel owners here and abroad found the pot of gold when a stellar array of agitated actors began outbidding each other for the best they had to offer. An actor's ego is such that only the best will do, and I can't help but chortle to think how many "bests" were sold from each kennel.

Some, including my father, went to Europe – even then the "If it's imported it has to be good" syndrome prevailed. Daddy, being one who felt that if two is good three must be better, brought back from England two Setters and a Pointer … His rationale for this splurge being that after the show he could use them for hunting. The discrepancy in this logic was that he had never held a gun in his hands and frequently was found setting the leg of an injured field mouse. But they did fit the country squire image.

My knowledge of the resultant exhibition is based more on lore than recollection. I have a kaleidoscopic impression of frenzied preparation culminating in a production calculated to make Ben Hur look like a 4-H project.

Anyway, that is how I got into dogs. They must have been pretty good specimens, as their show career didn't stop there, and the apple orchard was soon converted into a kennel.

Although we always had a few Pointers, it was to the breeding of Setters that my dad gave his heart. I don't know if any of them ever went Best in Show, but there were an awful lot of ribbons and trophies displayed about the house.

A child's memory idealizes fact, so perhaps my right-to-present-day comparison is suspect. I know I thought them the most beautiful creatures on earth. Though my father never used them for hunting, his friends did, and they would come back from a day in the field, and one bath and a few days later would be off to honors at a dog show. I remember their great mental and physical soundness. I remember gleaming coats that served their function without interfering with the purpose of the dog. I don't know if the term "dual champion" was used, but I rather think it was the norm rather than the exception.

Pages have been filled decrying the overemphasis on coat for the show ring. Coat has become synonymous with condition. Smooth or wired-coated dogs have suffered less at the hands of the hair fetishists and among them, and more frequently, are to be found dual champions.

There are few lovelier sights than a well put down Setter or Spaniel … if, under the glorious coat, is a dog so structured that called upon he can serve his function.

Professional handler Teddy Young put it well, I thought. Shortly after his beloved top winner Cocker bitch, known to the world as Bunny, formally as Ch. Sagamore Tacoa, owned by Peggy Westphal, made her earth-shattering leap out

Babbie Tongren with her daughter Pat.

of the whelping box into the show ring, I overheard someone refer slightingly to her abundant tresses. To score their point and bring Teddy to his knees they asked, "How far would she get in a field with all that coat?" To which Teddy answered, "Not far, but cut it off and she could go all day." That is what it is all about.

If the basic structure is that of a useful Sporting dog, and is implemented with the glamorous furnishings required for today's show dogs, the cake is iced and no harm done. If those furnishing are to cover a multitude of sins in the name of show dog, the Sporting dog has no right to his name.

In one of my first Sporting assignments I awarded Best of Breed to an Open bitch over a number of top-winning specials. Aware that I would be accused of being a giant killer I hesitated, but the heat of the day proved the undoing of all those glamour kids who one by one wilted on the vine. When the smoke cleared and decision time came, only the bitch remained ready to do her job, as her over-bedecked rivals were dropping by the wayside. The discomfort of the day had been as acute for her and she had come up from the classes, not sitting on ice cubes until the moment of entry.

Somewhere along the line I have fallen into the pit of the show dog as opposed to he who is created for a purpose with the physical and mental ability to fulfill it.

Before I resume my autobiographical saga, I must interrupt my ramblings to mention a jolt apropos of the above.

Judging a dog show last year, I saw laid out in front of me prima facea evidence of my protest. I was doing another Sporting breed – a short-coated variety many of whom were better than average. To my joy, when specials came in I was delighted to see a particular bitch to whom I had previously given my heart and all the honors I could bestow at a show. A typical, balanced, muscled girl who went on to win the Group and I understand has done enormously well since. I suspect that so engrossed did the owner become in the show career of her bitch that she had lost sight of what the quality had been that lent her brilliance. Instead of the forceful, muscled girl that outshone all, I was presented with a lethargic schlep up and down the ring. When I put my hands on her it was somewhat like plunging them into a bowl of tapioca. It broke my heart but I had to refuse her.

This started to be the story of how I got into dogs, and don't think you are going to get off that lightly. I still have "Life with Mother" to cover, which is even more bizarre.

As is the way with many theater people, my parents' marriage dissolved and with it the kennel of Sporting dogs. After a lengthy court tussle over my custody my mother lost – and so I grew up with her to guide me.

As was befitting her station she had not been allowed to enter the hale and hearty tweedy male world where words such as "bitch" are used.

Whatever her motive, Josephine was not one of the world of lady-like achievement. Her curiosity was piqued and she elected to try her hand at the world of dogs. Her mother had already begun an interest in the breeding of Pekingese, which I am sure lent impetus to Josephine's determination.

And so began a career unparalleled, which I will take up at a later date.

Sitting here, letting the past flow by me, I am inclined to think the question should not be, "How did you happen to get into dogs?" but rather, "How did you happen to stay in dogs?"

Chapter 19

Looking Back

My love for Paul Lepiane, the first editor of *The Afghan Hound Review*, has to be boundless – why else would I have agreed to do this? Agree I did, albeit reluctantly and only after some thrashing and screaming and suggesting some I felt are more qualified than I.

"Everyone knows," I said, "that my memory is both faulty and geared to my own convenience." "Everyone knows," I said, "that it has been at least ten years since last I sat through an entire specialty, and six years since last I saw any of it." To no avail. "Do it!" he said. Thinking to jog what memory I have, I unearthed my catalogs, only to find the most recent being 1973.

Now, I appeal to you: Does this sound like one qualified to do a déjà vu piece on parent-club specialties? The best I can offer is a kaleidoscopic jumble, a patchwork of memories, mostly out of context, some tender, some bitter. Nostalgia is at all times unreliable, so I refuse to guarantee the accuracy, but these are my mementoes. Fortunately there aren't many who have been around long enough to question the authenticity of them.

With more intent to amuse than inform, I warn you it may be hazardous going, so watch out for the potholes and hidden curves – but come join me in my trip down memory lane. I think it only fair to warn you that the specialties that get my unequivocal approval are only the ones that I won; they were masterpieces of show giving and judged by splendid arbiters.

I have in front of me the briefest of notes about the earliest days from 1940, which marked the inception of the Afghan Hound Club of America shows. My notes say that the very first one was judged by doctor Eugene Beck whose Best of Breed was Ch. Tanyah Sahib of Cy Ann; just noticed that there is no Best of Opposite Sex, strange. Again in 1941, no Best of Opposite. Judged by Dr. Combs, Best

Marion Florsheim with Ch. Rama of Chaman of the Royal Irish. *Photo courtesy Sighthound Review/Bo Bengtson*

of Breed was owned by Dr. Gertrude Kinsey and known only as Ch. Hazar.

The next three were all won by Charlie Wernsman's Ch. Rajah of Arken, judged successively by Dr. Kinsey, Muriel Boger (later president of AHCA) and Venita Oakie. I must pause here to say that one of my few regrets is that I never met Venita Oakie, which was the merest happenstance. She was flying back to California from New York to be a guest of honor at a cocktail party to which I had been invited, when she was killed in the plane crash. I guess it was a thing of splendor to see when she judged, young and beautiful with a Hollywood glamour that carried over into her ring presence.

They tell me that she and Marion Florsheim, although good friends, were archrivals in the ring, and that the whole dog show would flock to the Afghan ring when these two glorious creatures were fighting it out. Picture it: Marion, who was an accomplished pilot, in fact flew for the military, would swoop down out of the skies, always with make-up intact and well-fitted flying suit, a sharp little cap on her blond curls and the most discreet jewels. She would alight from the plane with Rana of Chaman or Rudiki by her side, pose for the photographers and proceed into the fray with Venita, who I am sure was equally well prepared. Sure would like to have seen that encounter. They were both judges, and I don't know for sure, but I assume they showed under each other. I am happy to say that at Marion's last assignment she gave me the group at Bucks County with Karli, a win I treasure, as I have always regarded her as the mother of our breed in this country. One of my sadnesses is how often I have mentioned her name to a current exhibitor only to draw a blank look in response.

Anyway – no show in 1945 due to restriction on travel because of the war. (Now we know what it takes to cancel a dog show.) The next five shows were absolutely fascinating, at least statistically. I don't know who else was there. I just know that if you weren't one of the chosen few, you might as well stay home. Every one was won or judged and turns out taken by Leah and E.F. McConaha, who won the first three with Ch. Karach of Khanhasset, then judged the next two which were won by Marjorie Jagger (later Lathrop) with Ch. Majara Mahabat, who was sired by the McConaha's dog. There seems to have been two shows in one year, so that Bob Boger, whose wife Muriel was very big at the time, and Charlie Wernsman, who was also a strong influence, also judged. It is all very confusing, but there certainly seems to have been a tight lock on Afghans by that chosen few.

In fairness to the Afghan crowd, I must say that at all dog shows, wealth and influence played a dominating part. Going over old catalogs one finds some of the old kennels with as many as 90 dogs entered, which were transported, with an army of handlers, in box cars, so it just must have been a monumental power struggle among the rich and social. Presumably there were some good dogs among the hoi polloi, but I wonder if anyone ever noticed. It is fun to note that Sunny Shay sneaked in a couple of times but only got as far as Winner: She must have been a blow to the elite.

I don't know how it happened, but in 1950 the reins evidently slipped from the hands of the glory crowd, because the judge was not only not one of *them*, but a tradesman, a professional judge and a Jew! It was he who is revered by all of us who knew him as the embodiment of all that is superlative in dog men, Mr. Dog Show, Alva Rosenberg.

It is here that my personal recollections can be called into play. Although I had attended two or three of the early shows, it was purely as a spectator and totally ignorant of anything except the beauty of the Westchester Country Club grounds and the wonder of the exquisite dogs. By this time I had wet my show-going feet as an exhibitor with some success in California, and returning to New York had entered Kurki ben ghaZi, who went second in the Open class in spite of my total inefficiency with a lead and my absolutely unknown face.

Well, let me tell you, all hell broke loose! All the wrong people won. That Alva

Ch. Turkuman Nissim's Laurel.

Rosenberg didn't seem to give a tinker's damn about whose social position was whose, and never once did he appear to run a Dun & Brad on the people in the ring … Heresy! Although all the right people were present, the end of the day found Sunny and Ch. Turkuman Nissim's Laurel in the winners circle. Caftan, as he was called, had been imported by Sol Malkin from England. I have always felt sorry for the people of today who never saw him, a superb-moving black dog with white feet that enhanced his floating gait. He had a white blaze, and thank God that wasn't considered the unforgivable fault it is today or he would have been lost and that would have been unthinkable. I must say that the blaze varied at each show, according to how much time Sunny had to change it. In those days there was no great fuss made over cosmetic changes, and Max Factor did a flourishing business at the shows, so no one really cared.

A slight irrelevancy – one of the most memorable sights ever seen was Sunny and Caftan winning the Group at the Garden. Sunny, slim then, in a black riding habit with immaculate white stock and gloves and Caftan shining black with his white chest and feet. Talk about bringing the house down!

1951 was unique in that there were three judges, Cy Rickles, Mel Strann and Dick Herbold, interesting because there were no more than 60 dogs entered. The bulk of the chore fell to Cy Rickles, whose Winners Dog was owned by

Lem and Shirley Ayers, who were very successful theater impresarios. The dog was Oakvardon Zorach of Venita Oakie's breeding. I note that Eva Gudgeon of Canada was there, a queenly and impressive lady. She owned the wonderful Ch. AsriHavid of Five Mile. Oh, yes, those days saw some glitter and glamour long since lost. We had such social luminaries as Consuelo Vanderbilt, Mrs. Carwithen French (now Louise Snyder), many theater folk, Charlie Constabile whose Las Vegas interests were well known, Dr. Bill Ivens who, to my mind, was a dog man unsurpassed but whose judging approval was revoked by the AKC for reasons that were shaded but called by them his veterinarian business. Thank God, that body has been immeasurably reformed. Anyway, it was a classy affair.

Cy gave the final nod to the California dog, Ch. Blue Arabis of Kuverya. I well remember the audible gasp that went up when Paul Mountz, the handler, made a well-timed entrance into the ring. We were all lined up waiting when in they walked. I for one recall dropping my lead, and everyone stopped dead. The color blue has become commonplace now, but in those days it was entirely unseen, and I want to tell you that dog was powder blue. His furnishings were probably black, but everyone who saw him will swear they were navy blue. For that time his coat was immense, and he showed like a king. I have no idea of his qualities as an Afghan, but be they great or faulty, his impact was such that no one really cared.

1952 … Now we get to the good stuff! The judge was Alex Scott, about whom all that was known was that he had imported the first pair of Afghans to this country, that he was then kennel manager for Amelia White's Kandahar kennels in New Mexico and that he was a Scotsman. My mother and I had three entered from our first litter: Karli, his sister Sinceri and brother Kujur. Karli by then had been shown three times and amassed nine points, including Best of Breed and Group 2nd at his very first show in Philadelphia. Although he was unbeaten in the breed until that time, we had little hope for a victory at the specialty. Marjorie Jagger Lathrop, the undisputed queen of the breed, had announced the initial presentation of Majara Mihrab, whom she had held back to make his debut at this specialty. It never entered our minds that this much-vaunted successor to the crown of Majara could possibly be defeated. He was then three years old, and our foolish, gangly, sparsely coated Karli was but 18 months. Loathe as I am to shorten this saga, let it suffice to say that Karli was Winners Dog and Mihrab was Reserve. Kay Finch's beautiful Crown Crest Carioca was Winners Bitch.

There were 19 specials entered, which included all the top winners of the day and our Ch. Kujur, who finished in five shows. The ring at the Henry Hudson Hotel was fairly small, so thinking to be considerate I took Karli aside and sat in a ring-side chair to give room for all those famous dogs. I couldn't believe it when

Ch. Crown Crest Zardonx, two-time AHCA national specialty winner, in 1957 and '58. *Photo courtesy Sighthound Review/Bo Bengtson*

Mr. Scott crossed the room and told me to take Karli out to the center of the ring. In his delicious Scotch burr, he said softly, "Take him out, young lady, and make him look good – make him look Goddamned good!" The rest is history. The icing on the icing is that Mr. Scott told me later that my nearest contender was the red dog shown by Deo Emory, Ch. Kujur ben Ghazi. Karli finished going Best of Winners the next day at Westminster with his sister Sineri Winners Bitch.

I guess I have always had trouble understanding the rationale of the parent club, because in 1953 we drop to one judge for the whole shebang, Dr. Combs again. I don't remember too much of this one, except that Sunny went Best of Winners and Best of Opposite with a beautiful cream, Zala of Grandeur. I guess she is so bright in my memory because I had a chance to own her and like an idiot refused, and Sunny wisely grabbed her from the lady who was giving her away. She was lovely! This time Mihrab triumphed, and again Majara reigned.

In 1954, Chris Shuttleworth, a well-respected former handler from California judged and Majara was still in the driver's seat. A Mahabat son was Winners. As in most of my catalogs, I gave up marking after dogs, being too busy socializing, so I don't know what bitch won. The record-holding showman, Ch. Taejon of Crown Crest, was Best of Breed with the flair that he and Kay always put into their appearance.

Now let's talk about 1955. Believe me, it was something to talk about! Not because the dashing Dr. Eugene Beck judged again, not even because it was a show that has never been equaled. At that time we were lucky enough to count among our ranks Betty and George Skinner. George was then a well-known TV personality and lent us some of his expertise and facilities to really give them something to remember. With the help of Bob and me, not exactly new to the ranks of theater, he decided to do it up brown. Dr. Beck was so handsome and had the most divine soupçon of Hungarian accent, so almost every woman in the place forgot to care what ribbon he handed her. (I think I was gladder about having my picture taken with him than I was that the picture was for Best of Breed!) Charlie Ruggles, then famous motion-picture star, was an old friend of my father's and had owned Afghans, so I persuaded him to present the trophies. We innovated a "Honor Parade," which has since been done at some all-breed shows, including Westminster, but

Ch. Sahadi Shikari, 1963's winner.

at the time was unheard of. George had persuaded the electricians from his show to come up with their equipment, and from somewhere he produced music. We had every top-winning dog lined up, Blue Boy, Caftan, Tamerlaine, Taj Akbaru, our three, Marjorie's current ones, Louise French Snyder had hers and every one else who was anyone. As each dog entered the darkened ring, he was picked up by a spotlight and to the sound of music. Mr. Ruggles read off his name and a brief history. We would then circle the room and Mr. Ruggles presented us with a rosette. It was show biz, but what's wrong with a bit of "show" in "dog show"?

1956 was judged by darling and now deceased Teddy Hays, who gave Kay Winners with Ruby. I was pregnant at the time, so Kay was kind enough to handle for me. Aside from this, it was Majara breeding primarily. Best of Breed was a screamingly popular win by 15-year-old Patty Leary and her pretty black-and-tan bitch Ch. Lala Rookh of Estioc, bred by the then active O'Connors. Everyone resented her

Richard Souza showing Ch. Sterling Silver, 1967's winner.

winning. Her weekend was untarnished, she won best Jr. Showman the next day at Westminster – a sweet child who is still around occasionally, making me feel antique with her grown children.

1957. Sissy Froelich judged, Joan Brearley went Winners Dog with Crown Crest Jesi Jhaimz and to round out a triumphant day, Kay was Best of Breed with Zardonx. Bob got Best Puppy and Reserve with ben ghaZi's Kaman. I hate to say it, but I was pregnant again. I remember this because being ineligible for Westminster, Kaman was taken home by some friends and escaped on the Merritt Parkway. Twelve hours later Bob found him lying regally on someone's lawn in Darien, Connecticut, having been seen crossing the parkway numerous times. It leads to wonderment that Bob just happened to be going down the right street at the right time when that crazy puppy lay down to rest.

1958. This time Anna K. Nicholas presided in her ever soft spoken and thoughtful way, and again Zardonx won.

1959. Cy Rickles once more at the helm. This time honors were divided between Grandeur and Estioc, and guess who was Best of Breed? Shirkhan triumphed looking even more marvelous than when he had gone BIS two years earlier at the Garden. He was grown up now and all majesty.

1960. As I was judging Westminster the following day, I didn't attend and only know that Ch. Crown Crest Mr. Universe won under Bob Boger.

Babbie showing ben ghaZi's Maracaibo under judge Frank Hardy at the 1967 Afghan Hound Club of America national specialty, where he went Winners Dog.

Ch. Shangrila Pharahna Phaedra, shown by owner-breeder Gerda Kennedy to AHCA national specialty Best of Breed in 1970. *Photo courtesy Sighthound Review/Bo Bengtson*

1961. All-rounder Percy Roberts was the judge, and once again the winners were Majara, either directly or from the line. The ultimate star was Holly Hill Draco, owned and bred by the Kauffmans.

1962. Dr. Waskow was presiding. By this time Shirkhan's influence was firmly established and all the top winners, except for Best of Opposite, who was the unforgettable Eljac's Dragon Lady Dureigh, were all sired by Shirkhan. Talk about sticking to type! Best of Breed was Lois Boardman's Ch. Akaba's Top Brass, who proved to be a strong influence on the breed.

My personal memory was of the dog I elected to show, a Shirkhan son that I had inherited and, I may add, one of Shirkhan's lesser efforts. We all adored the dog personally, but had to admit he was to say the least faulty. Anyway, after the judging, in which Willy ignored us completely, he asked me why I had elected to bring this particular specimen to him. "Because," I said, "he is the only Afghan I have ever owned who doesn't sit on the furniture." Willy looked at me thoughtfully for a minute and then replied with great logic, "Then next time bring some furniture for him not to sit on, because he ain't going to win no other way."

1963. Color was reinstated this year in the presence of the judge, Kay Finch. I wish a few more of us dared to be as brilliant as she. Best of Breed was Ch. Sahadi Shikari, bred by Joan Brearley, a truly exquisite Shirkhan son, owned and shown by Dr. Earl Winters. "Sheik" was one of my all-time favorites; at times he could be a bit apprehensive but his elegance was unsurpassed. He went on to compile an enormous record and I have always felt did a great deal to save Afghans from the "Hairy Yaks."

1964. The 25th national specialty, and appropriately the judge was the illustrious Mrs. Sherman Hoyt, famed as a Poodle breeder and the first woman to go Best in Show at Westminster, which she did with her owner-handled Standard Poodle Duc. She was of such elegance and glamour that no one has replaced her. Famous for always showing in pristine white gloves, she is still as regal as ever and talks of returning to the show ring. Many are not aware of her early interest in Afghans, but her Ch. Rudika of Blakeen went BIS at age 11. Blakeen was Hayes Hoyt's kennel prefix and bore some influence on Afghans early on. Her Best of Breed was Ch. Tajmir's Redstone Rocket, owned by Patty Sinden and J. Fanti.

1965. Alys Carlsen, long a leading light in the AHCA, a former president in fact, judged and her Best of Breed was Ch. Majara Muzaffar.

1966. I was in California and all I know is that Stanley Dangerfield of England judged and put up Ch. Ammon Hall Judas.

1967. Here we go again, and those who don't like it, get your own column. This one is mine and I am going to say that to me and some others this was one of the best-judged specialties: no one can argue the consistency of type. Judged by the late and so lamented Frank Hardy, dubbed "Mr. Hound," Winners Dog was ben ghaZi's Maracaibo. Winners bitch was Rajah's el Bint, both bred by Dureigh Kennel and closely related. His Best of Opposite was Jambala's Timbala of Grandeur, a Shirkhan daughter out of Alsi ben ghaZi, and his Best of Breed the wonderful Ch. Akaba's Sterling Silver, who doubled up on Shirkhan. Frank saw his type and honored it, and the end results were a miracle of consistency.

1968. Cy Rickles again was major domo, and this time it was Mandith Kennel, of Judy and Herman Fellton, who dominated. Winners Bitch was Mandith Golden Fleece and Best of Breed Ch. Dahnwood Gabriel. I don't think that anyone who was there will ever forget "Gabby." In the truest sense of the word, Gabby was not my kind of Afghan, but when he stomped into that ring, with Mike Leathers, now the very respected and popular Michele Billings, being towed along in his wake, you knew that here was a dog to be reckoned with. He was all power and showmanship, and when he made his presence known, you'd better pay attention. I have never seen such a vibrant force. Today's popular term, macho, describes Gabby. He demanded and got his recognition … whew, what a dog!

1969. Again unable to attend, I was pleased to find out that the very beautiful Ch. Coastwind Gazebo was Best of Breed under Louise Snyder.

1970. Herman Fellton and Eunice Clark shared the honors; however, someone decided to facilitate things by having dogs and bitches run concurrently in adjoining rings. I want to tell you – confusion reigned. Everyone with two entered was going mad vaulting ropes and taking in the wrong dogs. I hope they don't try that one again. The top-winning bitch Ch. Shangrila Pharahna Phaedra was Best of Breed. It was the first time many of us had seen her and Dr. Kennedy, and they were a moving machine, going together in unerring sync. Phaedra was a real queen who regarded the win as her just due.

From here on, all is down hill as far as my memories go. I either was judging another specialty that day, or due to boredom left halfway through, but for whatever reason I am not really qualified to comment. I did see some of the 1973 show and was so impressed when Rod Quevedo, realizing that the heavy carpet was giving the dogs electric shocks, carefully touched the brass railing before putting his hands on the dog, a nice man. I remember Dr. Waskow selecting the so very elegant El Cid for Best of Breed and the crowd cheered.

I didn't attend any further shows until 1975 and then only saw Bob Stein, whom I regard as one of our better Afghan judges, do dogs and thought again that here was a man who sought and honored his type and no one can ask for more from a judge. I was off to judge a Dachshund specialty, but the record tells me that Anne Clark did Best of Breed and gave it to that nice dog with the awful name, Ch. Lipizzan's Big Red Machine.

Because of an enforced absence from the scene for a couple of years of illness and then the roving specialties, I am not prepared for further comment. Besides, anybody out there reading this was probably around themselves and doesn't need my reminiscences. If I seem to have allowed ennui to rob me of my loyalty to Afghans, it may be because I don't see many of them anymore.

Chapter 20

It Pays to What?

One of the great advertising campaigns of all time has been the promotion of the Volkswagen into the position it currently enjoys in the Phillips System of Automobile popularity. There was an enormous obstacle to overcome in selling this car to the American public, much of which was reluctance to further the economy of a nation that made lampshades out of people. Madison Avenue's soft-sell genius not only overcame a two-war prejudice with such endearments as Beetle, Super Beetle and the Bug, but catapulted the VW into its current role of darling of the American hearts … the funny-looking little car that's a member of the family.

The buying public of the U.S. is advertising oriented. We are led, bludgeoned and influenced at every turn by the news media, radio, TV, magazines, throwaways, blimps and skywriting. Like giant spiders, the PR men decide what we are to buy, and dutifully we buy it.

Though I pride myself on being a free-thinking individual, I am dismayed to find that I am not immune to the insidious lure of the publicized product. Stopping to buy a disposable lighter the other day, I chose the Cricket, although its exact counterpart, selling for 50 cents less, was displayed alongside of it.

It would be fascinating to know how much the "All aspirins alike" commercials have boosted the sale of Bayers. According to the FDA, aspirin is a prescription and must adhere to standard, the 19-cent-a-hundred variety containing identical ingredients.

Expert promotion can sell ice cubes to Eskimos, but expert it must be. Not for nothing is Mary Wells paid exorbitant sums for her promotional ability. *[Mary Wells Lawrence was a ground-breaking American advertising executive. – Ed.]*

Babbie's daughter Pat with Ch. ben ghaZi's Zephyr of Mecca, a Silver Shadow son.

Nothing delights me as much as analogy, so hold your hats, here we go again.

Conceding that few dog people can afford to hire Mary Wells, I suggest the next best thing is to analyze the successful sales campaigns, then at random open any dog magazine and compare. If you can be truly objective, use your own ad as an example. Remember, you paid hard-earned cash for what in most cases is little more than an ego trip.

As a lifetime coward I am not going to risk tar and feathering by naming specifics, but honest to God I am looking at the following full-page ad in a national dog magazine. In large print so ornate as to be unreadable is an obscure kennel name heading the page. The picture happens to have been taken at a show by a professional photographer so the quality is adequate. We have dog, windblown owner and non-committal judge. Under this, name of dog – Dipthong of Nowhere Kennels. Who, we are told, continues his winning ways by going Reserve at the prestigious Boots and Saddles show in tough South Dakota competition. Next an enumeration of wins, the pictured Reserve being the triumph of his career … a ruffle of drums … Dipthong, a flashy, elegant, sound showman whose beautiful head and faultless movement have attracted the attention of judges from coast to coast. Under this somewhat slanted description, "Dipthing is at stud to approved bitches only"… name and address of owners.

As one whose only contact with Madison Avenue is 51 *[then the address of the American Kennel Club – Ed.]*, I claim no expertise in consumer relations, but I know a bummer when I see one! Sitting here, perusing this miracle of ineptitude, the serenity of my living room is shattered by the ghostly guffaws of ad men past and present.

It shouldn't take Young & Rubicam to tell us that in a publication of 250 pages, 40 to 60 percent of which is advertising, it takes impact to halt the back to front flip most people do with a magazine. Impact is the key word to success, the single factor that rivets the attention of the reader.

Rule #1 is simplicity. Since stories were carved in stone, "Boy meets girl, boy loses girl, boy gets girl" has been the skeleton around which best sellers have been wrapped, a basic, simple formula. A famous author told me that for every word that appears in print he had written twenty. The idea being, write the barest essentials and then amputate half of them.

In short, an effective ad should succinctly convey: A. what is being sold; B. Why it should be bought; C. Where it can be found.

Back to old Dipthong and his less-than-stellar presentation.

Presuming he is front runner for a future dynasty, why introduce the kennel name in Sanskrit? A one-inch banner heading in pedestrian, easy-to-read English type is going to implant itself in a lot more memories than something that has to be held upside down to read.

The Chinese make some smart remark about a picture being worth ten thousand words, and as usual they are right. The pictorial evidence of Dipthong's glory is adequate but scarcely loaded with impact.

Because it is the breed in which the flipper is interested, he may stop flipping to investigate, only to learn that this is Dipthong of Nowhere Kennels, presented by his owner, being given an inglorious award by an anonymous judge. So much for Dipthong. Flip to another page.

Rambling about a bit, I want to include a personal admonition as a judge. Contrary to popular belief, judges are people and as such are subject to human gratification and pique … anonymity is piquing. We can't help feeling that if a win is important enough to boast about publicly, then the judge is important enough to mention. Be there a man with soul so dead he doesn't like to see his name in print?

Here's the punchline … "Dipthong of Nowhere Kennels is at stud to approved bitches only." In most cases, "approved" means, "Can you afford the stud fee?"

Who in their right mind is about to ship their precious bitch to breed to a dog about whom they know nothing except his name and that he went Reserve someplace? Even if he swallows the bit about perfect movement, the most naïve breeder wants to know something about the pedigree. The average stud ad divulges little more than the name of the dam and sire. It is a rare thing that both parents are famous enough to need no further identification. A three-generation pedigree is not only good taste, but good business. Even back a generation or two, a celebrated name will catch the eye.

The fatuous text is a marvel of platitudes: "continues his winning ways." If every dog is really so replete with "winning ways," where are the losers?

Every triumph is gained at a "prestigious show." No matter the area, it's always "tough competition." Am I the only one who ever made an easy win?

The verbal portrait describes a paragon, "flashy, elegant, sound, beautiful head," etc. Fairly takes your breath, right?

The seed of doubt begins to sprout when we are advised that he has "attracted the attention of judges from coast to coast." This implies a pretty heavy campaign. How is it that all he has going for him is one Reserve?

In an orgy of arrogance I once ran a picture of a lovely champion bitch of mine. The only printing was her name, Apryl, my kennel and address. Of all the pages I have covered, this caused the most comment. Of course she wasn't at stud.

Cluttering up a sheet with a lot of superfluous adjectives and half-truths is guaranteed to invite apathy, not inquiries. An easy rule of thumb is, "Impact, simplicity and relevant facts."

I don't know how Messers BBD & O would handle puppy sales, but this appears to be a classic example of DON"T.

On another page, same illegible heading. The picture in this case is a do-it-yourself job, of a cut-down bitch lying in a whelping box surrounded by an indeterminate number of what appear to be laboratory mice. A flowery description of each puppy follows. Then, "Available to show homes only."

What on earth does that mean?

That every one of those mice is unequivocally a show dog? Hogwash!

We know that the mother is old flashbulb eyes, pictured; of Dad we learn he is their current contender. No further background is offered. Buying pigs in pokes went out with the Edsel.

How much more effective would be an attractive picture of the parents, a three-generation pedigree and a list of sexes and, if possible, color.

Impact – Simplicity – Relevant detail

More complex is the promotional campaign of a show dog, calculated to catch the eye of judges. The theory being that repetition gains recognition and a psychological edge. An interesting note: For whatever reason – wealth, intelligence or experience – campaign ads are by and large more professionally handled than those peddling tangibles.

Here's the zapper:

To keep my observations non-partisan, I chose another national magazine. There are seventeen full-page ads, representing a variety of breeds, each winning an impressive award. They are complete with handler, judge, record, etc. ... and not one identifies the breed!

No one has to be an all-rounder to recognize a Boxer or a Poodle, but there are some breeds that resemble others, and new ones with which the general public is not totally familiar. Dog books have an esoteric appeal and the subscriber is usually informed on dog matter, but there is the potential owner who is wise enough to read one for the purpose of joining the sport or trying a new breed. There are even judges who out of their own group may find a degree of confusion between some lookalikes (not me – I know everything).

When General Motors sets out to sell a new car, no one has to guess if it's a Cadillac, Buick or Chevrolet ... they bloody well tell you.

The summation of this dissertation might well be ... next time your ego needs a trip, talk to your mother. Next time you set out to sell something, think about how the pros do it.

Impact – Simplicity - Relevant facts.

Chapter 21

Required Reading

As one whose youthful involvement with academia was fraught with frustration and ultimate rejection, causing my mother's hair to gray and the Department of Education to admit inglorious defeat, I am less than qualified to discuss the polemics of mandatory reading. Jane Austen was not to my liking, and I couldn't possibly straighten out all of those names of Tolstoy's. Dr. Johnson and La Rochefoucauld had some neat stuff to say, but I couldn't handle all those Greeks.

So, for reasons important only to me, I have my own list of the written word that I wouldn't be without. Here is a partial list (and if you'll hang in there, I'll get to the subject at hand). I don't know home plate from the fifty-yard line, but I treasure Red Smith. Ben Hecht, who wrote with a telegraph pole dipped in blood. Anything Mencken chose to say was a monument of grace and economy. Nathan's reviews. Tom Payne, who skipped centuries and talked to us. Rostand, Priestley and Mark Twain, Margaret Halsey's "With Malice Toward Some." Salinger's "Catcher in the Rye." Some Vonnegut, Lucius Beebe's manipulative wording device and unabashed snobbery in "The Big Spenders." Wolfe, Wilde and Woollcott. Anytime Lillian Hellman wants to tell me something, I'll listen. Anybody at the Round Table for wit. John Housman and Elizabeth Barret, but not Browning. I love words, but Edwin Newman infuriates me, how come "Nobody talks good but him"?

Anyway, I have left out so many, but few of those gifted folk read dog magazines so I needn't worry about wounding anyone's feelings. Hopefully (take that, Mr. Newman), I haven't wandered away from my intent.

It is certain that Richard Souza will be astonished by his inclusion in this exalted company, but he needn't be. I prefaced this rambling file of heterogenia mentioning required reading and here is where we find Richard.

It is sad indeed that we of dog persuasion become so immersed in our particular segment of the world that expansion is unique. So, it is doubtful that Richard Souza's trenchant interview in a recent issue of *Afghan Hound Review* will reach more than some Afghan breeders and Hound judges. Excepting Lyon's "The Dog in Action" and a few other books that are of interest or value to the fancy, as a whole most of the pages we see are of esoteric appeal. Although Richard's words are directed to Afghan breeders, they would be of inestimable value to anyone proposing to enter our domain, no matter the breed.

A word about Richard Souza, as I know him.

Richard Souza has never bored me!

Our friendship has spanned some years and many miles. We have agreed and disagreed, with freedom and security. We talk in words and never in euphemisms.

Richard is a man of impeccable discernment and unrelenting scorn of the shabby. He reflects pretentiousness and delights in tilting those who practice it. He can level with a word those obsequious grovellers who vie for his favor. His dropkick is a thing of beauty when bringing to the ground those who try to impress him with the wrong things for the wrong reason.

I know he will writhe when I speak of his sensitivity, but I did say, "as I know him." At a time in my life when I felt little but pain, Richard reached out; he has understood anguish when decency demanded it be unspoken, and I wondered how he knew. He will hate me for this … but not for long.

The clarity of Richard's mind is analogous to dropping a pebble in a stream of clear water: You can follow its path to the bottom, and he has laid it all out for you to see.

My bedside table is heaped with books that for one reason or other I consider important to read, and so too often there isn't time for all the dog magazines that are sent to Bob and me as judges. Sometimes it is a back to front slip, and then they are discarded for want of leisure hours. When I saw Richard's interview I took it along on a trip, and as Bob drove I read it aloud. There was a great pile of "I wish I'd said that" that went on.

When I got home I reread it, mentally rejecting the specific referrals to Afghans and individual dogs and applied it to many breeds and much of the philosophy to other areas, but we are talking about dogs, aren't we?

Babbie in the ring with Richard Souza in an undated photo. The dog is Ch. Coastwind Abraxas, later the all-time top sire.

Because I feel it is important that as many people as possible consider what he says, I will take the liberty of quoting freely without the confines of particulars.

Although the interview is with Richard, no small credit for the success of Coastwind Kennel is due to the unwavering dedication of Mike Dunham – a fascinating private man of many facets. Without positive assertion I suspect that some of the providential decisions have been his.

Before I go one step further, I salute Richard's inclusion of luck in his story, because too many people get carried away with their own omnipotence and tend to forget that without the illusory Lady Luck – baby, you got plenty of nothing!

I have filled reams in protest of the division of "group dogs" vs. "breed dogs." I have thrown myself on the floor, hollered at the rug that the gap is widening and blamed breeders, calling out that if all that judges have presented to them are true-type dogs then that is what they will recognize. Richard also happened to be a lovely specimen of his breed, but his priorities are such that his interest lies in breeding his concept of the true-type dog. If they happen to become big winners in the Group ring, I am sure he would enjoy that, but it is the specialty wins of which he speaks with pride.

He talks of learning from others, of one lady who was the daughter of famous impressionist Ernest Lawson and who he says gave another dimension to his thoughts. In her day of breeding, pendantry bore no part and nothing was absolute. Today we all know our failures. How well I remember when we were breeding dogs that people who just happened to be passing (when you live in Bloomfield, nothing is "just passing") would call and want to "come and pick our brains." Hogwash! They wanted to come and bore us into oblivion with endless tales of their triumph in the match ring. I can't remember any who ever really posed one in-depth question as to how we arrived at our conclusions. None so much as ever glanced out a window at the dogs that they had professed such interest in. Richard tells of talking to another successful breeder and asking her why she had done a certain breeding. She had never been asked that before. "If you are serious about breeding you owe it to yourself to provide all the positive input you can, to help formulate your own ideas."

If you were interested in building a church pew, would you not ask the advice of a cabinetmaker? Yet we take something as fragile as blending components of a dog, the intricacies of which might well be comparable to throwing together a Boeing 747, with the willy-nilly approach of a stroll in the park.

Richard speaks of the over-emphasis on individual parts and likens it to the dissection of a M1 rifle. He speaks of pontification of seminars and the reams of type all dedicated to the standard, most of which are so intent on the tree that the forest is blurred. Standards are meant to be guidelines, not absolutes. There are priorities and trends to be considered and should we find a dog that is the standard physically, there is the mental posture. If anyone ever found a dog who put it all together, there would only be one dog at every dog show.

When asked about change, he responded, "Change started the day natural selection ended. Wherever there is individual choice, there is going to be some change. What I'm concerned about is concepts of breeders and judges. What most people call change is really influence." "Any prepotent sire or line influences the breed." He says that people were screaming about change in the 1930s and '40s, and will be ever after. "The gut issue with me is still the attitude of the Afghan. It plays such an enormous part in making him the king he deserves to be. There aren't any kings around. The kingdom is overrun with commoners."

On the omnipresent question of shoulders: "The theory that a 45-degree angle is functional for every dog has been set aside. There is more latitude than this in what makes efficiency. The muscles, tendons and ligaments are as important as the angles. It is these components that create the 'relating' of one part to another. Their function is to hold all the parts together and in place when moving or standing. The muscles make the parts move, acting on impulses sent from the brain. Furthermore, for every muscle that goes in one direction to move a limb, there is another working in opposition. Remember the axiom 'For every action there is an opposite and equal reaction'? Any weakness anywhere in a muscle can cause a dysfunction. This is also called balance – and it is the balance that makes for good movement – the Total Dog – the parts, muscle, tendons and motivation."

"I've seen judges go to great length to make an issue of the shoulder set alone. Not only do they not usually find the best dog, but they reveal that they don't really understand front assembly at all. I think it is time to take issue with things. I do it myself, but I believe in having a damned good grasp of what I am taking issue with."

On movement: "A beautiful dog standing still doesn't mean much to me if he can't move. All the parts come together in movement, and it's then that the best evaluation of the parts can be made."

Evidently, Coastwind has a reputation for being difficult to deal with, "it's their way or the highway," to which he responds: "Don't you think that any person with strong convictions runs the risk of being labeled 'difficult'? I don't give a damn what people say or think if they can validate it. Our dogs are in the position they enjoy because of the support of great breeder-judges, and it is on the strength of their support that my own convictions are based. I expect anyone who comes from a position of authority and speaks on behalf of their breed to be able to make as valid a claim. Opinion by itself is not authority. Saludos, Amigos!"

In its way, this has been an exercise for me, by removing specific referrals to see if Richard's words were really as objective as I had thought on first reading them. They are.

Chapter 22

Honesty, Decency and Respect

Some wise guy once said, "All good things must come to an end." There is much truth in this hackneyed old bromide. For after all, isn't this how adages live, in truth?

The euphoric cloud of sweet persuasion that has borne me aloft for an unlikely measure of time has, to put it crudely, bottomed out. Having often been called to task for what some have termed my sharp tongue or barbed wit, I have made a conscientious effort to avoid cynicism and allow my dimples to show. A gift for the unfrocked phrase is a dangerous talent, its victims find it unforgivable and friends are wary lest they be next. So my typewriter has dripped treacle and the bright side shone undimmed. That is, until now …

Would you like to know what has shot down my resolve to be all things to all men and turned my thoughts from nobility? Well, even if you wouldn't I am going to tell you, because it concerns you and everyone else whose energies and demands are of the world of dogs and the sport of showing – man, that is using a term loosely!

I have only just terminated a telephone call and, I may add, with an ear-shattering slam. Gathering my cudgels about me, I headed for this writing machine to vent some spleen that has been moldering long enough for want of venting.

About this phone call … No ordinary, "I think I'll ring up Babbie and chat" call – this was a toll call. Let me add quickly, when you live in Bloomfield, Connecticut, any call is a toll call, but this was a healthy, long-distance afternoon call from the far reaches. Initiated by one whom it would be stretching a point to call a friend, an acquaintance at best and one who I can't remember ever having phoned me before. Once the identity of the caller was established she told me her present whereabouts. I was incredulous, my brain rampant with curiosity. What conceivable emergency could have summoned me? The amenities were soon dispatched and my curiosity alleviated. It seems that this anxious correspondent felt it her duty to let me know that she had just been told by an unimpeachable source that a large and prestigious spring show was "rigged" for a certain well-known exhibitor to win, not only the breed but nothing less that the Group as well. What happened to Best in Show she didn't say, but the Group was a sure thing.

My immediate reaction was to utter an obscenity and hang up, but good sense dictated that I try to get to the root of this rot, and some more of her money. Pretending great compel I egged her to detail, which of course she was only too pleased to provide. It took practically no coaxing to pry from her that the unimpeachable source was the owner of the predestined winner, no less, whom she claimed was telling "everyone" that the dog could not lose under these judges.

Exerting a manly effort to control my nausea, I asked why she was telling me all this. My kennel now is comprised of two Smooth Dachshunds, so there is no way that I could be personally affected, even if it were true. Well, it appears that I was but one on a lengthy list that she and her well-meaning ilk were contacting. Dictated by sheer idealism, theirs were shining swords raised against the scourge of politics and their mission to see that the breed judge would draw a pitiful entry, thus humiliating her and slapping her dirty little fingers publicly. Although the caller knew that we no longer show dogs, she wanted to impress upon me the importance of warning away all with whom I might have some influence.

Reminding myself that there was too much at stake to indulge in the pleasure of cutting this impertinent twit to size, I tried reason.

"If what you say is true, what is the rationale behind the owner of this star-touched dog spoiling it for herself before the fact?"

"Because she wants to scare away the competition." "If what you say is true and the win is a fait accompli, why is she in need of scaring anyone off?" "Because she wants to be sure that another dog won't be there." "If what you say is true, why is she worried about this other dog?" "Because the judge has already put this other dog up." "If what you say is true, why are you playing her game for her by keeping away the competition?" …and so it went on, ad nauseum.

I don't know if I succeeded in dissuading this offensive little scud from further damage, but I tried. It wasn't until she had hung up that I permitted myself the luxury of a few well-chosen phrases as to her manners, her morals and the marital state of her parents, and then I headed for the typewriter.

It is to you out there that I make my plea. I have served my time and paid my dues in most areas of dog shows, my credentials are impeccable, so please listen to me! The issue here is not that coveted show, that much-analyzed dog or even those particular judges.

I am going to interrupt myself here to interject some personal observations about the breed judge. Though I can't claim lifelong friendship, she is one whom I admire as a woman and a sincere student of dogs, certainly a well-qualified judge of hounds. I have never heard her integrity deprecated – and surely this is a deprecation – until now. There is no doubt in my mind that whatever dog emerges victor does so simply because it was the dog and nothing but the dog that she deemed most worthy.

Of the Group judge – a man who has been involved in dogs all of his life, and his parents before him: He is respected and admired throughout the world; a bright gentleman. Now do you really think that one so versed in the intricacies of the absolute is going to be so indiscreet as to compromise himself in front of the entire world of his peers unless he truly believes that this is a great dog? There are some whom the maker created in the image of a horse's nether end, who might be willing to stand up in front of the world and demonstrate his persuasion, but believe me this man isn't one of them.

Anyway – the issue here is honesty, decency and respect. What unimaginable provocation could persuade you to denigrate anyone, and a stranger at that, in such terms as "liar" and "cheat"? … Think about it. Without our good name we are nothing, yet the most God-fearing who pride themselves on the generosity of their soul, who give pennies to old beggar women and never speak ill of the dead will deal in such epithets as "rigged, politics and fixed," delighting in their filthy gossip mongering. There is no writ of habeas corpus to justify these words that fall so trippingly from their tongues while they gleefully shred a person's reputation. How difficult is it to save the ark of reputation from the rocks of ignorance, and ignorance is the kindest motive to which we can attribute this moral devastation. More often the ruthless demolition of another's good name is motivated by an egocentric reluctance to bow to a superior dog, or even to admit the judge's right to think it a superior dog.

There are some with their excuse prepared well ahead so that when the dust settles they can smugly assert, "See, I told you." Many years ago, a lady then considered unbeatable announced that her loss was a premature certainty because – beat